becoming YOU

becoming the person God made you to be

PETER SONDERGELD

Foreword by Ed Welch

Becoming You: Becoming the Person God Made You to Be

Copyright © 2022 by Peter Sondergeld

Published by:

    Peter Sondergeld Ministries

    11 Moffatt St, Toowoomba, Queensland, Australia.

All rights reserved.

No part of this publication may be reproduced, stored in a retrieval system or transmitted in any form or by any means, electronic, mechanical, photocopying, recording or otherwise, without prior permission of Peter Sondergeld.

Unless otherwise indicated, Scripture quotations are from The ESV® Bible (The Holy Bible, English Standard Version®), copy-right © 2001 by Crossway, a publishing ministry of Good News Publishers. Used by permission. All rights reserved.

ISBN 978-0-6454034-0-4

To Angela and Jesus,
for their understanding and grace towards me
in my unfinished state.

Contents

Foreword i

Introduction v

1. Dehumanised 11

2. Dehumanised and stuck.....................................27

3. The cause of dehumanisation 45

4. The shape of dehumanisation 71

5. The true human 91

6. Becoming truly human 113

7. Interrupting rehumanisation 139

8. God's family—the place you become truly human...163

9. Becoming you 187

A final word 207

References 209

Endnotes 215

Foreword

Let's say you see trouble all around. You know that trouble has always been there, but somehow it seems more concentrated now. Extreme politics worldwide, climate crises, local uneasiness, anxiety, anger and more sneak into the details of your day through social media, vague anxieties, future fears, another fracture in a relationship. You have a keen sense that nothing is getting better. Then, at some point, maybe during a brief lull in the news cycle or an electrical outage that quiets the digital noise, you might notice that the trouble you thought was all *outside* of you is also inside.

You are not okay; *we* are not okay. Too much hiding, too much guessing at how to do life and relationships. We make it through the day on little scraps of meaning that are not enough to sustain us. Even when we know something about Jesus—the truest and fullest person—we struggle to absorb that knowledge in a way that leaves us with a settled wholeness. Scripture itself can feel like a collection of assorted pieces that we can pick and choose from. Perhaps if we could get ourselves sorted out, we would be in a better place to contribute to the world around us.

This book will help. Pete Sondergeld will be your friend and host. You will find him to be gentle, self-deprecating, wise, and fun.

He is always asking God, "Who am I?" and "Who are we?" (along with asking, "God, who are you?"). Then he listens and looks for answers. Some, you will discover, are sweet almost beyond words. Others will be contrary to all your expectations, yet they will make complete sense to your soul. Through it all you will overhear Jesus say that, though there are robbers of life, he is not one of them: "I came that they may have life and have it abundantly" (John 10:10). He is speaking to you. Who could resist?

Here are the two main themes of this book:

> **Scripture is one coherent story.** Knowing that is useful in itself. A great story is memorable. A bunch of arcane laws, holy wars, miracles that don't occur anywhere near you, and a few inspirational verses is not so memorable. Understanding the full arc of Scripture means you will be able to remember one great story, and you will want to tell it to your friends.

> **Scripture is your story.** Now this is where things get interesting. Imagine that someone has written your biography, and the entire book is accurate, insightful and energising. It makes you want to live as more fully alive. Since it is about you, you read every word. You laugh. You cry. And since God wrote it, and he has loving purposes for you, you are transformed. You become more you, in the very best sense.

You will find much that is familiar in God's telling of your story. But even what is familiar will sound new. When people speak on God's behalf you are accustomed to words that have grown tired, or even worse, ordinary. Think *sanctification, idols, blessed, holy, blood, sin, gospel*. They are all good and important words, but they have lost their vividness. These words and so much of the language you hear do not evoke clear, compelling images. You don't *feel* them as you might the pulsating low-end of a favourite band. But, make no mistake, God's telling of your story is very powerful to the point of being felt viscerally. You will notice that Pete works hard to render your biography in ways that you enter in and feel it. He wants you to catch the awe and amazement that comes when we truly hear God.

Welcome to a story that will leave you saying both, "yes, that's me," and "yes, that is who I want to become and am becoming."

Ed Welch

Introduction

You have a problem with your self.

So do I. We all have a problem with our 'self', the non-physical part of who we are. It's a long standing problem, one from which no one is exempt. You can trace it all the way back to the Garden of Eden and the fall of humanity.

Before the fall, humanity's self was quiet and content. It was like a child playing happily on its own, it was calm and didn't draw attention to itself. Then, on one fateful day, everything changed. When humanity fell into sin, the self fell with it—and it began to scream. The quiet, tranquil self of humanity suddenly became noisy, erratic and unruly. Those who were once truly human had been dehumanised, and the troubled self was Exhibit A.

Like a virus, Adam and Eve passed this troubled self on to all of their descendants, to you and me. We know what it was like for them, because we struggle with the troubled self too. We know what it is like to want to be great one moment and hide the next. We know what it is like to scapegoat others in an effort to be presentable. We know what it is like to make excuses in order to cover up our shortcomings. We know what it is like to manoeuvre and manipulate others so they will like us. We know what it is like to live with a fundamental dislocation between who we are on the inside and the person we project on the outside. We know what it is like to fear being known and to want to be known at the same time.

Once you know what to look for, you will see evidence of the troubled self everywhere. Start with social media. This is where people put themselves on display, a key place where the troubled self can be easily observed. Take a quick scroll through it and you will see a wide spectrum of the self. At one end, you will see those who are determined to be their authentic self, warts and all; at the other end are those who you know take multiple photos, flick through countless filters, crop, and digitally manipulate whatever they post. Then there are the likes, the views, and the comments. Although we can pretend we don't care, they often weasel their way into our psyche and mess with us. The last thing anyone wants when they post something personal online is silence. For many, digital silence has become the equivalent of being walked past, ignored. It is the worst.

The troubled self also appears in the terminology we use to describe our personal struggles. While we may not use the words 'troubled self' to describe our experience, we have many phrases and terms which lead us directly to it. We talk about self-hatred, believing in yourself, the need to forgive yourself. We describe others as narcissists, insecure, lacking in confidence, arrogant, self-obsessed, and people who need to give themselves a break. These and many others show up regularly in our conversations.

A troubled self can be incredibly hard to live with. Although it can operate normally at times, it is often painful, uncomfortable, and can swing wildly from one extreme to the other. The headaches it causes us spur us on in a quest for a cure—and there are many on offer out there. Maybe we think performance will help to manage our troubled self. We work long and hard to master skills that we (and our culture) believe will finally make us someone. Maybe, sick of being enslaved to the opinions of others, some of us manage our troubled self by declaring, "Enough! I don't care what anyone else thinks about me anymore!" Maybe we manage our troubled self using marketing—we project an ideal self rather than our true self. Or perhaps we fall for a different type of marketing, which sneakily makes a connection between who we are and what we own. If we have tried to manage our troubled self over the long haul and have not succeeded, we can end up tired and devoid of hope, settling for mere existence rather than the thriving we used to hope for.

We are not alone in our battle to manage a troubled self. In the last hundred years or so, a long line of mental health experts have stepped up to assist us. The most well-known American 19th century psychologist, William James, suggested self-esteem (a category he used to describe your assessment of your own value) was mathematical in nature. If you wanted to improve it, you either had to lower your expectations or improve your performance. Others followed him and promoted self-love as the answer to the troubled self. They encouraged us to control our self-talk and only think loving thoughts about ourselves. Eventually though, we discovered that self-love tends to cause many of the problems we are trying to resolve rather than fix them. The self-compassion movement taught us to be kind towards ourselves, countless books have been written to help us be our authentic selves (something which must be harder than it seems), and the recent adoption of Buddhism into secular psychological practice has recommended the abolishment of the self altogether. But while we can learn something from almost all of these sources, none of them gets the job done. We still carry our troubled self around with us.

Unfortunately the church hasn't always done much better at finding a solution to the problem with our self. Historically, the church has had too many moments where it has uncritically absorbed the culture rather than presenting a compelling and truthful alternative; the self-esteem construct and its remedy of self-love are prime examples. Then there are the times in the church when we have captured the truth about something but have struggled to understand or articulate exactly what we are all talking about. For example, we say we need to get our identity from Jesus, which is true, but we aren't always sure what that means or how to do it. Finally, the church can teach something true and right, but lets people down by the way that teaching is implemented. The truth may be good, but the mechanism we use to apply it is not so good. True statements about who we are in Christ abound in the church, but if we are left alone in our bedrooms trying to make ourselves believe them, then they will be limited in their helpfulness. We are not designed to stabilise the self on our own.

The reason why the troubled self is such a difficult problem is because it is a deeply personal one. Our problem with the self is not superficial; it is a problem at the very core of our being, it is a problem with who we are. Another way of saying it is: the problem with the troubled self is a problem with our identity. And who we are, our identity, is the operating system by which we live. If our identity is disordered then the way we live our lives will be too. We always live out of who we are. It's that simple.

Each purported remedy for the troubled self brings with it a particular understanding of the person. If you want to resolve the problem with the troubled self, or identity, you will need to have a resolution which fits the nature of humanity—it needs to align with the way we have been made. And this is where many of the approaches we've just looked at fall down. Scripture teaches that when God created humanity he hard-wired us to himself by creating us in his image. We are, by default, relational worshippers. And while this doesn't explain everything about us, it does explain the most important part.

Discovering who you are is not an independent quest; it isn't something you can do on your own. The only way to truly become the person God made you to be is to be closely connected to him. This is the way you have been designed. While sin messed with our identity and caused an interruption in transmission, Jesus made the way for us to be close to God and draw life and vitality from him again. You won't ever become your true self on your own. It just doesn't work that way. You will only become your true self as you become deeply connected to Jesus. It turns out who we are is more about who he is than we thought.

If you have tried to find your identity using any of the remedies I mentioned and they didn't work, this book is for you. If you are tired of doing it on your own, this book is for you. If you are tired of a noisy, unruly self, this book is for you. If you are someone who honestly sees your shortcomings and earnestly desires to live into who God has made you to be, this book is for you. If you are tired of living with a troubled self and you find yourself longing to be the person God made you to be, this book is for you.

I want to tell you a story, the story of Scripture, and help you to see how it is your story too. We will look squarely at the dehumanising effects of sin, the majesty of the true human, and walk along the pathway of restoration together. In the process, you will also need to look squarely at the messy details of your life. It will be uncomfortable at times, you can be assured of that. But don't worry; God will be there too, with lavish amounts of grace and mercy set aside just for you. After all, the dark places are the very places where Jesus' mercy and grace come into their own.

Don't expect God's work in you to be done by the time you finish this book. When it comes to your restoration, God intends on doing detailed, thorough work which will stand the test of time. While you can expect him to do some of his work quickly, it isn't the norm. He is a master craftsman. Expect his work to be gradual and careful. He knows what you need, and he knows how much you can handle at any one point in time. But be assured, he will finish the job, and when he does, everyone will be amazed.

The journey back to being truly human is a peculiar one indeed. God will lead you into new ways of living which will feel so right, so familiar, and so normal. They won't be mountaintop experiences which inevitably fade away; they will be new ways of living which feel strangely familiar, even though you have not done them before. Sometimes it will seem as if you are waking up from a dream. At other times, the pain and the panic of your dehumanised state will disorient you and obscure the way forward. Be sure not to give up. You don't need to know the way forward; that is not your job. It is Jesus' job. Your job is to stay connected to him. He knows the way.

Peter Sondergeld

1. Dehumanised

My wife and I have been married for over twenty years. Over that time, we have developed some relationship traditions, many of which are common in marriages. One of them happens every afternoon when we arrive home after work: we say hello, greet one another with a hug or a kiss, and then ask, "How was your day?" We have probably asked each other this question tens of thousands of times. It's a simple question, but don't be fooled into thinking it is superficial. We don't ask each other this question to simply gather information, but as an invitation to tell a story. What we are really saying is, "Don't just tell me the bare facts, tell me what they meant to you. Tell me about the good bits and the hard bits and what you did with them. Tell me your personal story."

The Bible is God's story. It begins with creation. In the first chapter of the Bible (Gen 1), we see the all-powerful, transcendent God bringing the earth into existence, Hollywood style. He creates everything out of nothing, using nothing but words. The action is dramatic and unlike anything we could imagine. Then the focus shifts. We get a second run through the creation account (Gen 2), but this time in close up. We see God getting personal with his creation, getting dirt under his fingernails. Everything is good and right, but not for long.

In the third chapter of the Bible (Gen 3) we read about the day when much of the happiness and goodness God created came to an end. It's a sad read. It was the day humanity, in the persons of Adam and Eve, turned their back on God and brought evil and suffering into our world.

Imagine sitting down with Adam and Eve at the end of that day and asking them, "How was your day?" I wonder what they would say. I imagine they would tell you straight up it was a bad day, and then correct themselves by saying it was the worst one ever. Perhaps they would tell you how the day started like any other. Things were in order. Shalom, "universal flourishing, wholeness, and delight"[1] was evident everywhere. There was no suffering or trouble of any kind. Then a crafty serpent entered the Garden of Eden and struck up a conversation with Eve (Gen 3:1). As she recounts the story she is visibly uncomfortable and you can sense her regret. She says, "If only I could go back and do it again…" She recounts how the serpent tricked her into disobeying God, how she ate the fruit she wasn't supposed to, and how Adam joined her. They describe the troubles which charged towards them and end in shock at the realisation that they had vandalised God's perfect world.[2]

Let's slow down and spend some time considering this day and the consequences which stretch through history, from Adam and Eve to you and me. It may have only been one day and one conversation, but like any fall into temptation, the speed at which it happened masked the far-reaching, often devastating consequences to come. There had never been a day like this before and there won't ever be one like it again. What happened on that day was truly horrifying.

Sin disorders

Sin corrupts and destroys what is good. Like rust on bare steel, leave it long enough and whatever was good will almost entirely disappear. The way sin attaches to good and corrodes, corrupts, disorders and destroys is plain from the opening pages of Scripture.

"In the beginning, God created the heavens and the earth" (Gen 1:1). His powerful word spoke it into existence. In the opening chapter of Genesis we read over and over again, "And God said ... And it was so ... And God saw that it was good" (Gen 1:9–10,11–12,14–19). He is the Lord of creation, and as he exercised his lordship and dominion, good things happened. Under God's hand, creation moved from disorder to order until he reached the pinnacle of his work—the creation of humanity in his image and likeness (Gen 1:27). God's creating of humanity in his image, in effect, hardwired us to himself, to live under him, depend upon him, and take our cues from him (Gen 1:28). Humanity was to fill the earth and exercise dominion over it for good, similar to the way God himself did.

God planted a garden in Eden for Adam (Gen 2:8). But it was more than just a garden; it was a temple, a place where God was active, present, and personally involved.[3] There, God got dirt under his fingernails and breathed life into Adam (Gen 2:7). He planted the garden and put the man in it (Gen 2:8). He brought animals to Adam for him to name (Gen 2:19). He created Eve and brought her to Adam (Gen 2:22). God took walks in the garden in the cool of the day (Gen 3:8). The presence of God is central in understanding the garden,[4] and it is his presence that helps us to see how the garden, with all of its rich symbolism, was the very first sanctuary or temple where God was "present in all his life-giving power."[5] It was good and it was life-giving because God was there.

When sin entered the garden in Genesis 3, what followed was the progressive dismantling of everything good in Genesis 1 and 2. The chapter opens with a crafty serpent engaging Eve in a conversation about God, his instructions, and his trustworthiness.

> Did God actually say, 'You shall not eat of any tree in the garden?' (Gen 3:1)

Eve was created to listen to God and her understanding of who she is, who God is, what is good, and what she is called to do came directly from him. The conversation with the serpent should have ended abruptly, but it didn't. And the longer it continued, the greater the dismantling of good. Eve answered the serpent's question:

> We may eat of the fruit of the trees in the garden, but God said, 'You shall not eat of the fruit of the tree that is in the midst of the garden, neither shall you touch it, lest you die.' (Gen 3:2–3)

God never said anything about not touching the tree, he only instructed them not to eat of it. Eve's additional rule flagged a shift in the way she viewed God; she no longer saw God as a good provider but as harsh, arbitrary, stingy and untrustworthy. So she distanced herself from him. The serpent replied:

> 'You will not surely die. For God knows that when you eat of it your eyes will be opened, and you will be like God, knowing good and evil.' So, when the woman saw that the tree was good for food, and that it was a delight to the eyes, and that the tree was to be desired to make one wise … (Gen 3:4–6)

Eve took on the role of deciding what is good. But that wasn't her job—it was God's. He is good and is the definer of what is good; Eve was created to discern what was good based on what God said. But she didn't. The conversation that never should have happened ends with Adam and Eve operating in direct opposition to what God had said.

> … she took of its fruit and ate, and she also gave some to her husband who was with her, and he ate. (Gen 3:6)

Adam and Eve weren't happy with God's definition of good; they wanted to decide what was good, and have it how and when they wanted it. They weren't happy depending upon God, they wanted to be independent of him. They weren't happy with merely bearing the image and likeness of God, they wanted to be God. They didn't trust him, they didn't wait for the good he had for them, and they preferred to listen to the voice of another who promised to give them what they wanted. It wasn't a minor misdemeanour done secretively in the bushes; it was brazenly done in his very presence in the garden.

Embracing dehumanisation

Immediately things began to unravel, and what was unravelling was Adam and Eve's humanity. Sin had struck at the very core of who they were. By detaching themselves from God, they had disconnected from what made them truly human. They had acted less than human, they were now feeling less than human, and they began treating each other as less than human. These glorious image-bearers were now falling short of the glory for which they had been made (Rom 3:23), they were hiding in bushes like little children, and were blaming anyone or anything they could for their situation (Gen 3:11–13).

In a moment, Adam and Eve went from innocent to guilty, clean to dirty, naked and unashamed, to naked and ashamed. It was a great fall. The place so perfectly suited to them, the other person so perfectly matched to them, the God who was so richly present with them … none of it fit anymore. It was gone.

It must have been like living a nightmare, emotions and trouble rushing at Adam and Eve like wild animals. They were once royalty, pure and righteous, made to reflect God and rule with him and on his behalf (Gen 1:26). Suddenly friends and family—God, Adam, Eve—turned into foes. No one could be trusted. A mad scramble ensued as they tried to regain what they had lost.

They began by sewing fig leaves together to cover up (Gen 3:7). Have you ever wondered how long it took? Were there tears? Was it frantic? Did Adam and Eve work together, or did they sew separately? However they did it, it wasn't enough. They had a problem which was more than skin-deep, a problem that had more to do with who they were than what they looked like. The covering up continued after God found them, this time in the shape of excuses and self-justification. But it didn't work. They would never be able to recover what they had lost.

Have you ever imagined trading places with Adam or Eve? You may recoil at the thought. There aren't many people who would be willing to bear the responsibility for bringing evil into the world. But what about the opportunity to taste what they had before the fall? Would you like to have experienced the purity, innocence, and flourishing that is shalom? Would you like to have taken part in that? Perhaps you would like to answer yes, but you hesitate. You hesitate because you know what happens in the story. You are well aware that knowing how good something can be makes evil's destruction of it more painful. You can understand a little of what it would have been like for Adam and Eve from your own experience of those pivotal moments when you were clean one day, dirty the next; innocent one day, guilty the next. Maybe you did it to yourself, maybe someone else did it to you. It doesn't matter so much how it came about. The grief of losing what you had before *that day* stabs you like a knife, just like it would have for Adam and Eve.

God questioned Adam and Eve and then handed down the punishment. Their sin was going to increase pain in childbearing, it would disorder relationships between husbands and wives, and it would affect the rest of creation (Gen 3:14–19). But the most severe punishment of all was death. The death God warned them about was stealthily creeping in (Gen 2:17). It had to. There was no other way. You can't turn away from the one who *is* life (John 1:4) and still *have* life.

Death – the ultimate dehumanisation of humanity

Physical death is a vivid expression of the dehumanising effect of sin. It unwinds humanity, the pinnacle of God's creation, making us dust again (Gen 3:19). It is the ultimate deconstruction of who God created us to be. But physical death, though delayed a little (it didn't happen on the same day as God had warned in Genesis 2:17), is not the only death we taste. Death is not just an event, it is also a state.[6] We can live in a state of death and spread death around us. How? By sinning. Sin and death are accomplices. Wherever you see sin, you will find death at work. Every time we sin, we scatter some death, a foreshadow of ultimate physical and spiritual death.[7] Every time someone sins against us, they scatter some death. Sin always kills, it always leads to death (Rom 6:23). It kills relationships, it kills people spiritually, it kills hope, it kills futures, and it kills people physically. In one way or another, we are always living in some way in the valley of the shadow of death (Ps 23:4).

The death Adam and Eve experienced that day was not physical (Adam lived over 800 years after the fall), it was spiritual and relational. Their actions that day brought about a breach in the relationship between them and God. This breach itself was death and was evidenced by their removal from the garden, the place where the tree of life and the rich, relational, life-giving presence of God dwelt.[8] To be disconnected from the presence of God is death and leads to death. You can't live without him.

Do you ever grieve the loss of God's presence? This may seem to be an odd question. You might say, "We live under the new covenant, we have the Spirit, God is truly with us" and you would be right. But you can be with God and have him living in you, but not really *be with* him. The disciples were physically with Jesus in the boat in the middle of the storm (Mark 4:35–40), but it didn't make any difference. They were in his presence, but not *in* his presence. Do you grieve the loss of fellowship with the Lord when you turn from him? Even for a moment? Do you grieve the loss of his presence? You need to. If you don't, then you don't really understand how good God is and how rich his relational presence is.[9] We need to walk closely with God, grieve when we are out of sync with him, and long for the day when he returns and takes us to the new creation with its garden and his uninterrupted presence (Rev 22).

But wait, we are getting ahead of ourselves.

Death gains momentum

Outside of the garden in Genesis 4, death and dehumanisation rapidly multiply. The very next chapter of Scripture after the fall describes how Cain, one of Adam and Eve's sons, murders his brother (Gen 4:1–12). It then goes on to record the song of bloodthirsty Lamech, who boasts about how his revenge is way more intense than Cain's (Gen 4:24). By the time we reach the account of the flood in Genesis 6, the process is complete, "The LORD saw that the wickedness of man was great in the earth, and that every intention of the thoughts of his heart was only evil continually" (Gen 6:5). Sin had not just affected the way people treated one another, it had corrupted every part of humanity down to the thoughts and intentions of the heart. When God first looked on creation, he saw it was good; when he looked after the fall, he saw only evil, all the time. Dehumanisation was complete.

As we move through biblical history, we see sin and its dehumanising effects running rampant. People lie (2 Kgs 5:22), commit murder (Exod 2:12), rape their half-sisters then discard them (2 Sam 13), take other people's wives and murder their husbands (2 Sam 11). Kings lead their people into the worship of idols (2 Chr 33) and sacrifice their children to them (2 Kgs 16:3). Everyone is busy doing what is right in their own eyes (Judg 21:25). Humanity continues to suffer long-term sickness (Mark 5:25–34) and death (John 11). It's a disaster.

This is life outside the garden.

Do you know what it is like?

Can you taste it?

Death reigns outside the garden

Physical death

For some of us, the taste of death is physical. You may have watched your loved ones die. You have looked death in the eyes, and you know firsthand how jarring it is. In old age, death can dehumanise those we love, killing them bit by bit. Maybe it is cancer, or dementia, or some other long-term illness. The one you loved is whittled away until only a shell is left. You tell yourself, "They had a good innings." But it is still hard. For others, death comes suddenly and quickly. "They were too young." "They had young children!" "They didn't deserve to go like that." Some aren't even born before they die, and we have cried as we held their lifeless bodies. Death, no matter how it comes at us, never feels right.

Sudden long-term suffering

Then there is the taste of death that comes at us without any rhyme or reason. There's no clear perpetrator, but you are stuck, saddled with some long-term suffering you didn't ask for and didn't want. Sometimes it feels so strong it could swallow you alive. Maybe it is the onset of persistent, long-term, physical suffering. Maybe it's a debilitating car accident, financial loss, or persistent mental illness. Whatever happened to you, it seems like night and day now. Before that day, all was light, and now it is darkness, a darkness you fear will be with you for the rest of your life. And you wonder how you can go on.

Being sinned against

Or there are those who sinned against us. We weren't randomly handed this death and dehumanisation, it was intentional. Whether they did it on purpose or out of cruel carelessness, either way, the perpetrator has a name and what they did dehumanised you. They manipulated you for their own ends, they took advantage of you, they ripped you off, they bullied you. You were merely an object for their sexual gratification or they verbally or physically abused you, and then they discarded you. Maybe it was long-term, grind-you-down, low-level ridicule, or maybe it was a one-off event. Their destructive action against you may be over, but you still see them at church, down the street, or at work, and that thing they did cycles through your mind, repeating the pain every time you see them.

It is in the past, but in so many ways it isn't over. For some of you, it is ongoing. Your humanity is persistently being eroded, and you die a little more each day.

The consequences of our own actions

Sometimes we dehumanise ourselves. Humanity has a reputation for doing this. As Adam and Eve did, we go after things that result in us becoming less-than-human. We become enslaved by things that are caustic to us: drugs, alcohol, the approval of others, sex, bitterness and revenge, and obsessive self-centredness to name a few. We have sayings that capture this human dynamic: "He eats like a pig," or "What an animal," or "You're a machine." When we become enslaved to our desires, we lose some of our humanity. No longer are we the glorious people, made in God's image; we become slaves driven by the fallen parts of our nature. Always drinking but never satisfied, we make bad decisions and are condemned to live with the consequences.

Victims and perpetrators

But we are not just victims. We are not just those who are on the receiving end of dehumanisation, we dehumanise others too. Our sin carries the same genetic fingerprint as Adam and Eve's. It wasn't long after the first sin that Adam turned on Eve. No longer "bone of my bone and flesh of my flesh", no longer one made in the image of God, she was now a scapegoat. Some argue it is society's or culture's fault. Society may be partly responsible, but society is made up of you and me and our next-door neighbours. Every time we sin against another person, we actively contribute to this depersonalising, dehumanising culture. No one is ever merely a victim. We are victims and victimisers, every one of us. We are the ones who bite and devour one another (Gal 5:15), with our words we have hated others in our hearts (1 John 3:15), we have treated others as objects, we have been bitter towards others, we are the ones who have taken advantage of others for our own ends. We are both dehumanised and dehumanising.

This is life outside the garden.

We groan

And we groan.

Groaning is commonplace outside the garden. Wherever there is death you will hear groaning, both from the dehumanised and those who love them. We were not made to be in a place where there is miscarriage, murder, selfishness, abuse, or ridicule. We were made for a place of shalom where God is richly present, a place where everything works properly. Sure, there are good things in this world but stop for long enough and you will see how much of the human experience is like an acid bath—it is caustic to your soul. If you have ever had a moment where you wanted to tap out on life, that's pretty normal. Groaning and being outside the garden go together.

The book of Psalms vividly portrays the experience of being human in a dehumanising world. There are lots of groans written on its pages. Just hear the groan in verse 10 of Psalm 90: "The years of our life are seventy, or even by reason of strength eighty; yet their span is but toil and trouble; they are soon gone, and we fly away." Ever felt like that? The Psalms have a powerful way of putting our groanings into words. This is one of the reasons they have been favourites of so many for so long. Listen to two other vivid groanings you will find in there:

> Greatly have they afflicted me from my youth, yet they have not prevailed against me. The plowers plowed upon my back; they made long their furrows. (Ps 129:2–3)

> My wounds stink and fester because of my foolishness, I am utterly bowed down and prostrate; all the day I go about mourning. For my sides are filled with burning, and there is no soundness in my flesh. I am feeble and crushed; I groan because of the tumult of my heart. (Ps 38:5–8)

Go ahead and read some other Psalms. About a third of them have some kind of groaning in them. And as you do, expect them to put some of your own groans into words. But take heart, you might also be surprised when you see how God interacts with those who groan.

A God who understands

God's list of punishments in Genesis 3 is strange. In a situation like this, we would normally expect the list to be all bad, but he mixes some good in there as well. He drops an amazing blessing in amongst all the curses. We see it in the cursing of the serpent: "I will put enmity between ... your offspring and her offspring; he shall bruise your head, and you shall bruise his heel" (Gen 3:15). Theologians call this the first gospel: someone, born of a woman, is going to come along one day and, rather than falling for the wily schemes of the devil, will decisively deal with him. The one to come will be hurt by the action he takes, but he will win.

God's rescue plan kicks into action from the very first sin, and it is more than surprising. We expect God to be flying off the handle at these stupid humans who couldn't get one simple thing right, and then rushing to get them out of his presence. "You bad people need to stay out there; I will stay in here!" But he is not the type to send us away, telling us we are not good enough for him. From that first mess, he had a plan to reverse it, and his plan involved him getting hurt.

As history unfolds, God's rescue plan gets clearer. He lets some of his prophets in on how it is going to happen, and what they say is startling. The saviour's appearance would be "marred, beyond human semblance, and his form beyond that of the children of mankind" (Isa 52:14). The Messiah surprised everybody. He left heaven, put on human flesh, and walked once again with his people. No one expected him to be one who would suffer. But he did. Just like it was in the garden, people rejected him (John 1:11). They didn't like him, they didn't trust him, and they didn't want him around anymore, so they trumped up some false charges, had him scourged and then crucified. On the cross, he wasn't just the victim of sin, he carried all of the sin which dehumanises humanity, and it dehumanised him. He was disfigured by us, disfigured by our sins, starting with the scourging and reaching a crescendo at the crucifixion where he carried our sins in his body on the tree and died. He knows what it is like to be dehumanised by sin.

We get God wrong

I often have conversations with my hairdresser about God. He has a Catholic background and, though he is not an active member of a church, he is sympathetic to the Christian belief system. On one particular day, we were talking about the Bible and I asked him what he thought about God dying on a cross. He responded, "No, I don't think that is true." I asked him why and he replied, "Because God wouldn't do that." I asked him, "Then what do you think God would do?" He answered, "He wouldn't come and sacrifice himself for us, he would come and take us out. He would get us." I changed the topic slightly, "Have you ever noticed how no one ever argues about whether self-sacrifice is good or not? Everyone, everywhere instinctively knows it is." He agreed. I asked him why it was the case. He didn't know. I followed up, "If everyone knows self-sacrifice is good regardless of who the person sacrificing themselves is, then isn't it reasonable to think it is part of the fabric of the universe? If it is part of the fabric of the universe, then why wouldn't it naturally follow for God to be like that?" "I guess he could be," he admitted.

We get God wrong. When we think back to the garden, we imagine him kicking humanity out, putting the curse on us, locking the gate, and then barking orders at us from a comfortable recliner chair. We don't really think he is with us, and we don't really think he knows what it is like for us. But that is a God we've made in our image (Ps 50:21). We think he is like us, or at least like our deepest fears say he is. But much to our surprise, this is not actually true. God really does understand. He is better than we think. Instead of kicking us out of the garden, shutting the door, and barking orders at us, he follows us out of the garden, locking the gate behind himself. We are not sent out alone. He comes looking for us and, in doing so, gets his hands dirty. He stands in the way of our evil and gets disfigured and dehumanised. He knows our pain, he's experienced it, he understands.

He gets you.

You can talk to him.

When life outside the garden is heavy and you groan, groan to him. This is the best groaning, the most human groaning. He understands us, he understands our troubles. This is what the Psalms teach us to do. Don't bottle it up, don't explode at people, and don't grumble. Tell him about your trouble, "pour out your heart before him" (Ps 62:8). Tell him about everything. He gets you.

The first step back towards being truly human involves you being honest about how sin and death have dehumanised you. The second step is talking to Jesus about it. It probably won't be fun. Looking at the effects of sin and death never is. I had many moments in the writing of this chapter where I wanted to look away too. But don't give in. There is one who tasted death for you (Heb 2:9) who you can look to for life (John 3:14-15) when the ravages of sin and death have had their way. Move towards him; in him is life itself.

> *His appearance was so marred, beyond human semblance,*
> *and his form beyond that of the children of mankind…*
> *He was despised and rejected by men, a man of sorrows and*
> *acquainted with grief; and as one from whom men hide their*
> *faces he was despised, and we esteemed him not…*
> *Surely he has borne our griefs and carried our sorrows.*
> *(Isa 52:14, 53:3–4)*

Scripture reading
Genesis 1–3

For reflection and discussion

1. What would it have been like for Adam and Eve the moment after they sinned? What changed for them?

2. Where can you see the vandalism of shalom (flourishing, normal operation) around you? Where do you find yourself longing for a return to shalom?

3. Where is death at work around you? How has sin dehumanised you and those you love?

4. There are five key expressions of death outside the garden. Which one do you know all too well? Which one do you feel the most acutely?
   a. Physical death—long-term physical illness and death
   b. Sudden long-term suffering—a life-changing traumatic event
   c. Being sinned against—a victim of other people's actions
   d. The consequences of our own actions—becoming slaves to things that dehumanise us
   e. Victims and perpetrators—we dehumanise others

5. Groaning is commonplace outside the garden. Wherever there is death you will hear groaning. Where can you hear yourself groaning?

6. When you groan, who do you groan to?

7. Which groans of yours don't get directed towards God? How would you tell him about them? What are some of the words you would use?

2. Dehumanised and stuck

I didn't understand what shame was until my late thirties.

It wasn't that I hadn't experienced it before then, I just didn't know that's what it was.

Can you see it in your own life? As fallen people in a fallen world, no one is exempt from shame. It is never about whether you struggle with shame, it's always about whether you can see it; you can certainly experience the effects of shame without knowing what it is. Some time ago I remember talking with a friend of mine about shame. He looked me in the eye and told me he didn't think he had a problem with it. I listened, nodded, and said, "Fair enough. Maybe you don't." Then God got to work over the next twenty minutes showing him all the places where shame was operating in his life—he wasn't as shame-free as he thought he was. If you have ever felt deep embarrassment after failure, then you know what shame is. If you have a habit of apologising too much, then you know what shame is. If you have ever felt dirty, unpresentable or unacceptable, then you know what shame is. If you have ever felt the need to cover yourself up, then you know what shame is. If you are a sinner, then you know what shame is.

As it turned out, shame had seeped into almost every area of my life. Once I had learnt what it was and how to locate it, I began noticing it all over the place. I could see it in the way I hesitated in social situations, worrying about what people would think of me. I saw it in my sleepless nights, lying awake in bed replaying the sermon I had preached that day, scanning for mistakes. I noticed it in the way I would overcompensate with pride when I was feeling uncertain about myself. It showed up in the way I responded internally to criticism—*they are right, I am wrong, I can't really have my own opinion.* But it wasn't all shame. Sometimes it was outright pride. The human tendency to swing between pride and shame is disorienting indeed—something we will look at a little later on in this chapter.

Shame alerts you to dehumanisation

Like a warning light on your car dashboard, shame tells you something is wrong. It alerts you to your dehumanisation. Sin always dehumanises people. It takes God's good creation and actively works to unwind it. Sin is the act that dehumanises people; shame is the dehumanised state. Shame differs from guilt in that guilt tells us what we have done, while shame tells us there is something wrong with who we are. Guilt convicts of sin. Shame condemns us as bad people. Shame is the stain of sin on our identity.

In *Shame Interrupted*, Ed Welch helpfully captures the connection between sin, shame and dehumanisation:

> Shame is the deep sense that you are unacceptable because of something you did, something done to you, or something associated with you. You feel exposed and humiliated ... You are disgraced because you acted less than human, you were treated as if you were less than human, or you were associated with something less than human, and there are witnesses.[10]

Shame is a kind of echo within a dehumanised person. It is the reverberation created when people operate less than humanly (1 Cor 15:34). In this sense, shame is appropriate and right—act less than human and you can expect to feel less than human. So far, so good. But in a fallen world, shame is far more pervasive than that. It isn't always connected to something specific that we or others have done; we can also pick it up from our connection to something less than human, or it can be a general, ongoing sense of worthlessness. While there is a healthy version of shame (Titus 2:8), most of the time it is unhelpful and lingers long after the sinful act has taken place. Sometimes we can't even work out why we feel shame, we just do. This kind of shame is not just an echo, but an evil one. The event which spawned it is long gone, but the feelings of dehumanisation continue to reverberate in our minds, sometimes for decades, or even a lifetime. It may have been a one-off event, yet shame replays what you did, or what someone did to you, over and over and over again. It is as though you live inside an impenetrable bubble, where the shameful emotions and words bounce around you, and you carry them everywhere you go. You see yourself as dirty, worthless, pathetic, a special case, undeserving of anything good. People tell you they love you and say encouraging things to you, but none of it makes it inside your bubble; their words hit the outside and slide off. Good things don't apply to you. It seems shame is the ultimate Teflon.

Shame's inception

Shame is insidious. It sneaks into our sense of who we are and stains the very operating system we run on—our identity. This is a large part of the reason why shame can be so difficult to pin down. It is just part of the way we do life. It seems normal to us, even when it is far from it. You probably have more of a shame mindset than you think. Much of what seems normal to you may not be normal at all but may be the result of the infection of sin and shame in your identity. Some of you get this. You have begun to see that the way you were treated was not normal. You operated—sometimes for years—as though the abuse, the ridicule, the people who took advantage of you, what it all said about who you are, was normal. Then somewhere along the way, you saw something different. Your understanding of normal was shaken or stretched.

One way of tracking shame down is by starting with its effects, then working backwards to the shame itself. Think of it this way: shame is a little like the mechanics of bonsai. Bonsai is the art of growing deliberately dwarfed trees in small pots. These trees and shrubs, which could grow into something tall and majestic, are intentionally dwarfed through pruning and the use of wires, to be a miniature version of the real thing. Shame is like this. It trims and truncates you. It trains you, not with wires, but with hopelessness and humiliation, until you are no longer a glorious person made in the image of God, but a dwarfed, miniature version of yourself.

Shame is not native to humanity. It is an intruder. While many of us have learned to live with it (perhaps some better than others) there was a time when there was no shame, and no dehumanised people (Gen 2:25). No one acted less-than-human and no one felt less-than-human. Sounds sublime, doesn't it? But it didn't last for long. When sin entered the world, shame came along with it. While the inner echo of shame in Adam and Eve doesn't appear on the pages of Scripture, we do see its effects in Genesis 3.

Shame's effects

Hiding

Immediately after the fall of humanity, we see one of the most obvious effects of shame—hiding. Shame causes people to hide. At the end of Genesis 2, Adam and Eve were naked and not ashamed (Gen 2:25), but seven verses later they're ashamed of their nakedness (Gen 3:7). Before sin, nakedness wasn't a problem, now it's a big one. So Adam and Eve got to work sewing fig leaves together to hide their nakedness. It wasn't just a covering up from God, because He is not mentioned at this point in the story. It was a covering up from each other; nakedness was not safe anymore.

Enter God. He was taking a walk in the garden in the cool of the day (Gen 3:8). What a sublime thought. In the afternoon, when the heat of the day had passed and the breeze was blowing,

God took walks in the garden, probably with Adam and Eve. But not that day. That day, the presence of the Lord was not welcome but was a threat. So what did Adam and Eve do? They hid in the bushes like guilty children. It would be funny if it wasn't so tragic. Did they think hiding in the bushes would work? Did they honestly think God wouldn't be able to see them in there? Shame leads us to do things that don't make sense. We do whatever we have to do to get out from under the gaze of others. When we feel less than human, that is the only thing that matters. In our minds, the ends justify the means, even if the means are crazy.

Hiding is not normal for true humans. Hiding is a sign the echo of shame is bouncing around in our lives. While we may not use fig leaves or bushes, we are all familiar with the impulse to hide and the odd ways we often go about it. Shame leads us to do things that make sense in the moment, but seem a little ridiculous from a different vantage point because they just don't do the job we want them to do. We buy the latest fashion or technology in the hope it will show we are valuable people. We work hard to be good at something our culture values, in order to compensate for the failure we feel. We drink alcohol or take substances to blunt the way we feel about ourselves, and it works for a time, but our shame is still there when we sober up. We seek physical affirmation and love from others but get only lust, leaving us feeling less human than before. And, sometimes, shame can mess with us so much we end up glorying in shameful things (Phil 3:19).

As the story in Genesis progresses, we see that the instinct to hide goes beyond the physical. When God asked Adam about his nakedness (Gen 3:11), another round of hiding took place, but this time it wasn't behind fig leaves. It was behind victimhood, excuses and scapegoating. Adam started by blaming the woman God gave him (Gen 3:12), then Eve blamed the serpent (Gen 3:13). Their efforts to hide behind the failure of other people led to them blaming God himself. After all, it was he who gave Eve to Adam, and he was ultimately responsible for letting the serpent in. This is classic shame. We know this strategy; it's in our playbook too. We know we have blown it, and we know it says something about who we are, but instead of going to God for help, we play the victim and blame others in an effort to maintain we are a good person.

This may come as a surprise to you, but the people who know you well can probably see what you are up to when you hide in your shame. They can see right through most of your sneaky strategies. Often the hider is the last one to know, or at least the last one to admit it. Some time ago, God helped me to see an area of my life more clearly. It was quite a revelation for me. In the light of what I had learned about myself, I decided it would be a good thing for me to go home and tell my wife all about it. The thought of telling her about some of my internal strategies made me nervous because I would be giving her the information to see me and know me in my darker moments. If I told her, then where would I be able to hide? I would be exposed. I would feel naked, even though I was still fully clothed. Eventually, I sat down with her, gathered myself and let her in on some of my secrets. She responded by saying, "Yeah I could see all of that. That's not really new to me." She wasn't being patronising or unloving. Quite the opposite. She had seen all of the mechanisms I had employed to protect myself and had been loving me anyway. So we got to talk about something we both knew about but had never discussed—and it was wonderful. In the end, I felt more deeply known and more deeply loved.

In the game of poker, a 'tell' is a subtle mannerism that gives the other players in the game insight as to what you have in your hand. You can only discover someone's tell by watching them closely and getting familiar with them and the way they play. Helping someone struggling with shame is similar. If you want to help a hider, work out what their shame tell is, and then speak love, grace and mercy into it. In order to do this, you will need to get close to them and pay attention to mannerisms that show up at the same time as shame is operating. One of mine used to be saying sorry. I remember doing a talk at a counselling conference in Sydney and a good mate of mine came up at the end and said, "That was really good, mate, but you just have to stop saying sorry." He was right. My shame was loud. I didn't feel good enough, lots of eyes were watching me, I felt out of my depth and not worthy to be doing the talk, and I hid behind saying sorry. It didn't work. He spotted it and he moved towards me to interrupt it.

Fear
Another effect of shame for Adam and Eve was fear. It was the driving force behind much of the behaviour Adam and Eve engaged in after the fall. And it wasn't just any fear, it was the fear of being known. After God asked where Adam was, he replied by saying, "I heard the sound of you in the garden, and I was afraid, because I was naked, and I hid myself" (Gen 3:10). Adam had lost some of what made him human and he knew it. He and Eve had turned from God and sinned, becoming less than what they were created to be. They were unacceptable, and the fear of being seen by God in that state ruled them, so they hid. There are some parts of trying to hide from God which make sense (even though it's impossible). After all, you would think that there is no more dangerous place for a guilty, dirty sinner to be than near a holy, righteous God. But that is not the only risk for the shame-filled person. There is a sense in which shame can make us walk away from goodness. We can feel so unworthy that we avoid the good, either because we feel we don't deserve it or because we fear the good will only serve to highlight our imperfections and uncleanness even more. But I wonder what would have happened if Adam and Eve had gone to God after they had failed and told him they had messed everything up. What would he have done? But our normal experience, a mixture of guilt, shame and fear tends to repel us from God rather than propel us towards him. Fear is shame's accomplice—without it, shame loses much of its power.

Many of you would be able to relate to the fear Adam and Eve experienced, the fear of being seen and known at our worst. There is no more vulnerable place than this. But the greatest fear of the shame-filled person is not the fear of failure, which has already happened; it is the fear of our failure being exposed and people rejecting us as a result. The one thing worse than feeling shame and not being known is feeling shame, being known, and being rejected. That is the worst.

But it gets more complicated. In a fallen world, we don't just have to wrestle with our shame and struggle with being known; we have to contend with the very real possibility, indeed the likelihood, that there *will* be some people who reject us as a result. The reality is we simply cannot guarantee the way people are going to respond to us. Obviously, the best place for a shame-filled person to be open and known would be in a perfect world, where people's reactions could be guaranteed, where we knew they would be for us no matter what. But where we live, in a sinful world, being known deeply is risky. Many of you have experienced this personally. You opened yourself up to be known and people mishandled and mistreated you. You shared something about yourself, and they used it against you. Now, whenever you have the opportunity to share something deeply, the words *I will never do that again* race through your mind and you shut down, guarding yourself from being known by others. You feel safe, but you have to live with your shame. It's a terrible trade-off.

Relational isolation

Perhaps the most powerful effect of shame is the way it isolates people. When humanity put themselves rather than God in the centre, relationships were fractured. This is also what pride does. It puts the self in the centre and separates us from those who won't join in with our self-seeking goals. In sporting terms, it is an attacking play. In pride, we move forward and compete with one another to lay hold of what we want. Shame bears some of the hallmarks of pride but is about defending oneself rather than competing with others. Pride is offensive, shame is defensive, but both end up with the same result—broken relationships and isolated people. We were made relational by nature, made to need God (Acts 17:28) and each other (Gen 1:27) to be who God had created us to be. Sin came and broke it all up, and shame followed, locking us in our relational isolation.

Shame builds a protective layer between us and others. In the beginning that literal layer was made of fig leaves and bushes, but other means quickly followed. The hiding we see in the fall is not just a turning to self-protection, it is a turning away from others. Adam and Eve hid from each other, and in the bushes they hid from God. This hiding from God was not just hiding from a judge or a sovereign, it was personal. Genesis 3:8 puts it this way: "The man and his wife hid themselves from the presence of the LORD God." The Hebrew word translated as 'presence' in this verse, can also be translated as 'face'—Adam and Eve hid themselves from the face of the Lord. This same terminology is used throughout the Old Testament to describe God and humanity's relational posture towards each other. Humanity hid from the only one who could help them, the only one who made them truly human.

God designed our relationality to be the pipeline through which help comes to us. It was the only way to be truly human, connected to God and each other. Before the fall, only good things flowed through the pipe. After the fall, both goodness and trouble flowed through it. Humanity, in our dehumanised state, decided the risk of being known and rejected was too great. The whole pipeline of relationality, that conduit critical to us being truly human, had to be shut off. In that moment we became insulated from both help and harm. This is where it gets tricky. Just because you shut yourself off from relationship doesn't mean you stop being relational by nature. What you end up doing is living a contradiction. In your heart of hearts, you want to be fully known and loved, but on the surface, you have a thick layer of insulation which stops this very thing from happening. You know you need to be rescued, but you can't bring yourself to open the valve which will allow the goodness to get to you. Instead, you live a life of "quiet desperation".[11]

In 2019, I was working with some men in a drug rehab centre. We were talking about the struggle with shame and the fear of being known. One of the men shared about the struggle he had in being open with his parents about the sordid details which led to him going into rehab. While he had good parents whom he could trust, it was difficult for him to share the mess of his life with them. Shame shouted at him to keep some of it secret. *Protect yourself! Who knows how they will respond? They will reject you.* He didn't listen to the shame, he told them everything, and they responded with love, acceptance and support. As he reflected on the experience of being known by his parents, he made this profound comment, "You can only be loved to the extent you are known." It blew me away. He was right. To be partially known and loved leaves the door open for doubt—*They wouldn't really love me if they knew the truth about me. They only love the bit they know, not the whole of me.* He lived out the reality that if you want to be loved deeply, you will need to be known deeply. That's how it works. You can't be loved without taking a risk. There is no other way.

To be loved deeply requires you to be known deeply, but to be known deeply requires you to take others to places that are the least presentable and most shameful. We don't always go there. While we want desperately to be loved, the fear of being known and not loved is powerful and often wins the day. This is what I call the ambivalence of shame. We love the thought of being fully known and fully loved, and we long for it, but it scares the heck out of us because we fear being fully known and rejected. So we end up stuck in the middle, neither fully known, nor fully loved. Isolated. Alone. Messy. Insulated from help.

A relational problem

Shame is an intensely relational problem. It came through a breach in relationship, and those who suffer with it do so under the gaze of others. When it comes to dealing with shame, humanity hasn't always brought the right tool for the job. Most of the time our remedies for dealing with shame are not relationally rich. Our culture says to deal with shame we should love ourselves, work on our image, accept and be compassionate to ourselves, guard our self-talk, ignore the opinions of others, or work hard to succeed. While some aspects of these remedies may be helpful, the truth is they don't go deep enough and they don't grapple with the essence of what shame is.

The church has worked hard to be helpful too. We have sifted through the Scriptures to find all the references which tell us who we are in Christ, and we have digested them and taught them to others. But they don't always stick; shame still seems to get the better of us. We think, "My identity in Christ must be true; it's in the Bible. I need to try harder to believe it." But it doesn't work. We don't seem to be able to believe it enough. The problem here is not with the Bible or truth itself, the problem is in the non-relational way we apply the truth about who we are in Christ. The church's approach to applying these truths often ends up being an independent task, as though we are willing ourselves to believe it will do the trick.

But we can't fix a relational problem without relationship. It didn't work for Adam and Eve, and it won't work for us.

What we need is for someone to come close to us, someone who is prepared to bust into our bubble of shame and know us fully. We need someone who will not recoil at our disfigurement or reject us when they see the real us. We need someone who will look upon us in our trouble, have mercy on us and love us. Deep down, we know we can't get out of this trouble ourselves. Performance won't do it—we've tried that. We need someone to come close to us in our mess and rescue us. We need mercy and grace, hand-delivered.

How God deals with the shamed

Genesis 3 is a busy, noisy chapter. If it were a scene in a movie, it wouldn't depict a serene landscape with a gently flowing stream bordered by lush green grass; it would be an industrial scene with welding, grinding, forklifts moving, steel clanging and cranes operating. In this chapter, good things are being torn down, people are fighting for what is not theirs, guilt is crashing in, people are blaming others, and calamitous curses are coming down upon humanity. It is a busy, noisy, cluttered scene, but in the middle of it all God steadily gets about his work. He is the key character in the story, and he is working to bring about his good plans and purposes in steady methodical ways. There is chaos in the foreground, but if we stop long enough to notice how God deals with shame-filled people, we will notice the hope mixed throughout this unfolding tragedy.

The first glimpse we get at the way God treats shame-filled people is found in the way he engaged with Adam and Eve. He called out to Adam, "Where are you?" Don't miss the beauty in this. Think of all the things God could have done. He could simply have left, never to be seen by Adam and Eve again. Or he could have gathered a bunch of angels together and exposed the humans—he knew where they were, they weren't hidden to him. He could have killed them on the spot. He had warned them about the consequences of disobedience. But he didn't do any of that. God is well aware of the tendency for confrontation to push people further into shame, so he didn't take any of these options. In the bushes, Adam and Eve needed God more than ever, but they couldn't get to him. They were stuck. So he went to them and busted into their shame bubble.

Did you notice the nature of God's question? Notice anything different to the way we often operate? God didn't lead with their problem; he led with their condition. They were lost. God didn't ask "Where are you?" because God didn't know where Adam was. He asked "Where are you?" because *Adam* didn't know where he was. We like to work from offence to condition, but God likes to work from condition to offence. His way draws us out of hiding. To have another human come close instils both fear and hope in the shame-filled person—it is both a threat and the possibility of rescue. But when God comes close, it is always about rescue. This is the way he deals with hiders: he comes close, talks tenderly, and draws them out. "I see you. I know your mess. I am here to help."

The second glimpse we get of God's heart for shame-filled people is mixed in with the curses in the second half of the chapter. We see how deeply God identifies with us. God promised that one day someone, born of a woman, would crush the head of the serpent. In that moment, God foreshadowed the day when Jesus, the son of God, would be born. He would be born of a woman and be like his brothers in every respect (Heb 2:17), living and working alongside them for 33 years. He would be despised and rejected (Isa 53:3) by his own people (John 1:11), the very people he created. They would trump up charges against him, beat him, and kill him by hanging him, naked, on a Roman cross. The Lord of glory would die the death of a criminal, and he would do it to carry our sin, our dehumanisation, our shame.

We can't say that no one knows what we're going through. In Jesus, we have one who comes close to us, who tells us he knows what it is like. He is not "out of touch with our reality";[12] he knows our struggles (Heb 4:15). He tasted our shame, and he didn't do it at a distance from a corporate box; he did it with human skin on (John 1:14). He clothed himself with human skin so we could be hidden in him (Col 3:3) rather than having to hide from him.

Towards the end of Genesis 3, we see a final glimpse of God's heart for shame-filled people—he makes garments of animal skin for Adam and Eve. This is an amazing role reversal. No longer are Adam and Eve hastily fashioning clothing together from flimsy fig leaves; God has taken on the responsibility of clothing them. He slaughters an animal and makes clothing to cover their nakedness. This is classic God. He takes a problem which was theirs and makes it his. He regularly does this. His heart is not to expose the shame-filled, but to cover them. The answer to our shame is not a return to the garden and the extreme vulnerability of nakedness, it is being clothed by another. Look through the rest of the pages of Scripture and you will see a similar pattern. We blow it, we try to fix it, we fail, and God takes responsibility for our mess. And his best work, the most amazing provision, was his son's death on a Roman cross. He carried our sin so we could be forgiven. He bore our shame so we didn't have to. He hung there naked so we could be honoured as royal children. God's heart is not to leave you exposed, dirty, or rejected.[13] He has made provision for you to be clothed in glory, clean and accepted.

God is better than we think

As Scripture's story continues, we learn more about the contours of shame. The book of Leviticus takes us beyond the category of nakedness and gives us a list of definitions of what is clean and unclean. One of the things we learn from this list is that shame is highly contagious. If you touch something unclean, you become unclean. While we don't live by the details of the Levitical framework anymore, we often still operate by the basic overall principles—stay clean, don't do anything shameful, and don't associate with anyone or anything which is unclean, because it will rub off on you. Shame often comes by association.

But for fallen sinners living in a fallen world, staying clean in a Levitical sense is easier said than done. Even if by some stroke of genius we were able to keep away from unclean things external to us (good luck with that by the way), it would only be a partial fix because that is not the centre of our problem. The centre of our problem is us and our hearts. "For out of the heart come evil thoughts, murder, adultery, sexual immorality, theft, false witness, slander. These are what defile a person" (Matt 15:19–20). In light of this, getting away from uncleanness would require us to get away from ourselves, and this is just not possible. Something is wrong, deep down. We can't get to a shame-free place through ultra-disciplined living; we need deeply personal transformation and restoration.

Some time ago, I was talking with a friend of mine. He asked, "Why doesn't God get rid of all the evil and suffering in the world?" It's a common question, one many of us have heard before. I answered, "Well, it depends on how far you want God to go. If you want him to get rid of all of it, then he will need to get rid of you also." My friend saw the problem. But discarding us or distancing himself is not the way God rolls. Instead, he associates himself with us. He comes close. Savour this for a minute. The holy God, the one who made you, the one you are meant to image, the one whose beauty is stunning, the one who is the polar opposite of you in your shame—yep, that one—*he* draws near to *you*.

And if shame is by association, Scripture teaches us glory is by association also. What we learn about God from the garden and the rest of biblical history is that he is not done with his people. He is one who associates with the shamed. Over and over in the covenant relationships God forms with his people throughout the Old Testament,[14] we read the following refrain: "I will be your God; you will be my people; I will dwell in your midst."[15]

Then our God comes, in the person of Jesus, and physically dwells in our midst. We get to watch him interact with the shame-filled, the outcasts and the failures. And to our great surprise, he is not repelled or disgusted by them. On the contrary, he seems to be drawn to them. We hold our breath as we watch him reach out and touch lepers and we frown as unclean women reach out and touch him, expecting him to catch their sickness. But he doesn't. To our great surprise, when God is involved, it works in reverse—he doesn't get sick; we get healed. He doesn't catch our shame; we share in his glory.

It turns out God is better than we think.

While we were busy running from him, he was moving toward us.

While we were busy protecting ourselves, he was busy providing for us.

While we were busy blaming each other, he was taking responsibility for our mess.

While we were busy hiding, he was signing the adoption papers.

To all who did receive him, who believed in his name, he gave the right to become children of God, who were born, not of blood nor of the will of the flesh nor of the will of man, but of God. (John 1:12)

Scripture reading
Genesis 3

For reflection and discussion

1. Shame speaks to you about who you are. It is the stain of sin on identity. What does your shame say to you? What does it say about who you are?

2. Where do you swing between pride and shame? What is it like for you?

3. Where are you trimmed and truncated by shame?

4. Three key effects of shame are hiding, fear, and relational isolation. Choose the most prominent one for you and reflect on its presence in your life.
   a. Hiding—Where do you cover up because you don't feel good enough? What does it look like?
   b. Fear—Where do you get stuck between the desire to be known and the fear of being known? How can you tell fear is operational in your life?
   c. Relational isolation—How does your shame get in the way of deeper relationships? Where do you feel isolated and alone?

5. What is one of your shame 'tells'?

6. What has shame robbed you of? What would it be like to live a life free from shame?

7. Where can you see the effect of shame in your relationship with God?

3. The cause of dehumanisation

Why?

It's a question we all ask.

It's a very human question.

Most of us began asking, "Why?" around two years of age. We were small, the world was big and there were lots of things to discover. We just needed to know why. Why this, why that, why … everything. If you were anything like most two-year-olds, then you probably drove your mum or dad nuts. They, like any parents, did their best to answer your questions, but in the end, there were whys which couldn't be answered, so they peddled out the classic question-killers like, "Just because," or, "It just is," or, "God made it that way." Sure, they tried to answer as many questions as they could but, in the end, they reached the edges of what they knew—an ongoing reminder we can know some things, but even then, we still walk in a land of mystery.

As we grew and matured, we continued to ask why, but the way we did it changed. It was no longer a single-word question, but took the form of education, reading books, running experiments, and learning from our mistakes. All these and more provided data for us on why things are the way they are in our world. Asking why is part of who we are. Our tendency to ask why assumes we live in a stable universe built upon cause and effect. It assumes there is a logic and design to the world we inhabit. If the universe were completely random, asking why would be meaningless. But because the world we live in has been designed and created by God himself, there is a reason and a purpose for everything. There are good answers every time we ask why.

Humanity's desire to know why doesn't stop at the study of nature, machinery, or science—we also want to know why we do what we do. You can see the evidence of this all over the place, from the explosion of psychological research, to the unfolding of a movie plot, to the need to find a motive for a crime in the courtroom—the whys and wherefores of human behaviour are important to us. We want to know what makes humanity go well and what causes us to malfunction. We are an inquisitive mob.

When we are going well, we tend to be less interested in why we do what we do, but when evil and trouble come close our need to know why presses in on us. Perhaps you can identify with this. Maybe something happened to you that you thought only happened to people on the news and it left you asking why. *Why did that person do it to me? Why did they enjoy hurting me so much? What were they thinking?* Or maybe you're reeling from something you can't believe you did. *Why did I do it? Why couldn't I stop?* These are real questions which loom large in the presence of real evil.

Other times, evil comes close via the 24-hour news cycle. Bad news gets delivered live into your pocket. It isn't just a terrorist attack in France that you hear about some time after the fact; it is a video on a screen in your hand, happening in real-time. You can feel your heart rate go up a few notches. It never used to be this way. Once upon a time, you would only see the news if you read a newspaper or watched the evening bulletin. Now it stalks you, and you have the anxiety to prove it. It is in your hands and at your fingertips 24/7. It brings the most notable of evil so very close, and it often leaves you asking why.

Something is wrong with humanity. No one argues with that. But what is the centre of the problem? What is the core human condition? *Why* are we like this?

By design

If you want to work out what is wrong with something, you need to have a clear picture of how it was made and meant to operate. Once you know what is normal, you will have a reference point for understanding what is wrong and how to restore it. If you look at almost any theory which seeks to diagnose and remedy the human condition, you will see the connection between design, diagnosis and remedy. What you think humanity is shapes the way you understand what is wrong, and the way in which you approach a solution. For example, if you think humans are mainly psychological, then the way they think will be central to understanding the problem, and correcting how they think will be a key part of the solution. If you see people mainly as biological machines, then you will see biology as central to the malfunction and the correction of biological imbalances as a key part of the solution. But if we truly want to understand what has gone wrong with humanity, with us, then we need to understand how we were created, and how we most naturally operate.

If you have been part of a church, then you would know one of the categories traditionally used to describe the core human condition—sin. We are sinners who have disobeyed God; we have missed the mark and have blown it. This was a strong emphasis in my sermons as a young preacher. You could sum up the core of most of my messages this way, "Sin was bad, we should feel bad about it, Jesus forgave us, and we should work on being good." But this approach always seemed to fall short of the transformative work I wanted it to do. I remember once when an elder in my home church complimented me after preaching, "You really beat me around the head today Pete." He intended it to be an encouragement, but it left me wondering. I can now see some of the shortcomings of that approach. The knowledge and conviction of sin are critical, but we need to remember that the general category of sin is more a behavioural label. It isn't something that helps us get on the inside of the motivations and mechanisms which produce it. It is more of a 'what' answer than a 'why' answer. "What did you do?" "I lied." "Why did you do it?" "Well, that's another story." 'What' tells us where we are; 'why' tells us how we got there.

God is committed to helping you understand what sin is and the underlying mechanisms that drive it. He designed you to operate in a particular way and he wants you to know yourself more so you can turn back to him more intelligently and apply his grace more specifically. We can expect to learn a lot about the way God designed humanity from the Bible. He is the one with expert knowledge about what is normal operation for humanity, what has gone wrong, and how to fix it.

Relational by design

God made us relational by default. We give ourselves in relationship to other people and things: other people, our pets, our phones, God, and so on. Look around and you will see people constantly giving themselves in relationship. When people's relationships are healthy, they do well; when they aren't, they struggle. One need not look any further than the well-documented effects of loneliness on humanity to see the centrality of relationships for us.

From the opening pages of Scripture, we see clues which point to humanity being relational by nature. In the beginning, the triune God created humanity in his image and likeness (Gen 1:26–27). Whilst the Old Testament doesn't define exactly what being made in God's image entails, we can identify some pointers to human relationality here. One of these pointers is the phrase 'image and likeness'. This same phrase is used later in Genesis to describe one of Adam's sons: "he fathered a son in his own likeness, after his image, and named him Seth" (Gen 5:3). To be made in the image and likeness of someone is to be part of a family and to bear the family likeness. And family is about people you are related to, it is about relationship.

As we move through Scripture, the basic relationality of humanity becomes more and more obvious. After the fall of humanity, God makes it clear he is not done with humanity and he is intent on doing relationship with them. But relationship between a holy, righteous God and sinners is tricky, to say the least, so he makes covenants with us. In simple terms, to make a covenant with someone is to enter into relationship with them, based upon particular, agreed-upon rules. While there are many covenants that God makes with humanity, the most well-known Old Testament covenant is probably the Mosaic covenant which God made with his people at Mount Sinai after he had rescued them from Egypt. The centrepiece of the covenant was the ten commandments, written on the tablets of stone (Deut 5:22). They were the foundational rules for Israel's relationship with God; think of them as marriage vows.

Every relationship runs by a set of rules—the closer the relationship, the more significant the rules. Break the rules and you break the relationship. In my role as a pastor, I have had a bunch of opportunities to walk with engaged couples from pre-marital counselling right through to their wedding day. One of the most critical parts of a wedding is when the bride and groom make their vows to one another. The vows are the joy-filled expressions of the couple's commitment. I enjoy this part the most. But imagine the couple makes these vows, heads off on their honeymoon, and then comes home and begins settling into normal life. A few days after they get home, the wife notices her husband writing out something on a sheet of paper. She doesn't want to intrude and so doesn't ask him what it is, but before long this sheet is stuck to the mirror in their bathroom. It is a copy of their wedding vows. She asks her husband, "Why did you put it up there?" He replies, "I just want to make sure I do what I said I would do." How would you feel about it if you were her? Is it admirable? Kinda. Is it a little unnerving? Yep. Why? Because keeping the rules misses the point. Complying with the rules of a relationship is not the main part of doing relationship—compliance is downstream of love. You can keep the rules of relationship without loving (Matt 15:8), but you can't love without keeping the rules. This is what Moses taught the people before they went into the promised land. He laid out the rules for relationship with God, the ten commandments, and then he told them how to fulfil them—love God with everything in you (Deut 6:5–6). Later on, Jesus would say the same thing—"You shall love the Lord your God with all your heart" (Matt 22:37). God calls us to love, the most personal and relational of acts, because it is what we were designed to do.

But while we are relational by nature, there is something unique about our relationality. We are not made to form relationships solely with others on an equal level to ourselves. There is a relational 'slot' in each of us which is reserved for doing relationship with God. This is the way God has made us. We always orient around and give ourselves in relationship to someone or something which occupies this God slot in our lives. We are relational but we are worshippers also.

Worshippers by design

Humanity was made to be oriented towards, and to behold, something great. In a general sense, this is true of all created things. The world and everything in it hinges on God. He is the centre. He made everything (John 1:3), he owns everything (Ps 24:1–2), and it all holds together in him (Col 1:17). Everything is made to orient around him, and everything points to him (Rom 1:20). But while we share some similarities to the rest of creation, humanity was designed to centre upon God in a unique way.

Let's revisit the Garden of Eden. Are there any signs Adam and Eve were worshippers from the beginning? Absolutely! You might remember, God planted a garden in the east of Eden (Gen 2:8), but it was not just a garden, it was a temple.[16] He created Adam and put him in this garden, the temple, to work it and keep it (Gen

2:15). Later, the priests had a similar responsibility in the tabernacle (Num 3:7–8).[17] Adam was created to centre on God, serve God, be with God, and image and reflect him (Gen 1:27)—he was the first priest. He was hardwired to God and hardwired to worship.[18] It was the worship of God which made Adam truly human, and it is the worship of God which makes us truly human (Exod 20:3–5).

In 2015, a research study into awe and its effect on the way people interacted with each other[19] asked a group of people to gaze at a towering stand of eucalyptus trees, while the control group looked at buildings. Soon after this, someone walked past and dropped a whole bunch of pens. Both groups helped the person by picking up some pens, but the people who looked at the trees beforehand were more helpful and consistently picked up more pens than the control group which had been looking at the buildings. Feeling small before something great does not destroy us, it changes us, because we have been designed to behold something great. If a towering stand of eucalypts—a mere shadow of God's glory—can make us more loving, how much more will we change in the presence and worship of God? This is what Paul celebrates in 2 Corinthians 3:18: "And we all, with unveiled face, beholding the glory of the Lord, are being transformed into the same image from one degree of glory to another." We were not made to be great; we were made to be connected to someone great.

Perhaps the most telling observation of Scripture when it comes to humans as worshippers, is that humanity never seems to end up in a worship vacuum. There is no neutrality when it comes to worship. When we stop worshipping God, we don't end up worshipping nothing, we end up worshipping anything.[20] Paul identifies this dynamic in Romans 1:25: "they exchanged the truth about God for a lie and worshiped and served the creature rather than the Creator." There are only two possible objects of worship—creator or creation. We worship one or the other. We were not made *to* worship; we were made *worshipping*. You can change the direction of your worship, but you can't shut it off. It is part of who you are. We are "unceasing worshippers and will remain so forever."[21]

Relational worshippers

Some time ago, I got to have an extended conversation with a man named Luke.[22] I was in a pastoral role and I had invited him to come in for a chat to get to know him better. He was from a very conservative Christian home, but he wasn't a Christian—he was clear about that. He knew I was a Christian and he was respectful to me, but he didn't disguise his dislike of Christianity. The Christianity paraded before him by his parents was hypocritical and unattractive to him. He, in contrast, was honest and authentic. We exchanged pleasantries in the early stages of the conversation, but before much time had elapsed, we got down to talking about what really mattered to him: bodybuilding. As he unpacked his life, it became clear to me his bodybuilding wasn't so much a passion as it was an obsession. His whole life revolved around it. He just had to be ripped (muscly and toned). He shared with me what his daily regimen was, the weightlifting sets he would do in the morning and the afternoon. He talked about his diet and his fear of getting injured because of how it would interrupt his pathway to the body he was working so hard to build. He revealed how often he stood in front of the mirror, shirtless, in extended self-admiration. We talked for over an hour. It was a fascinating conversation. He described his life and his commitment to bodybuilding in such clear and vivid detail.

On the wall in my office, behind where I was sitting, there was an A4 piece of paper which had a collection of different words on it. They were words that described the normal ingredients of a relational worship of God: love, fear, serve, sacrifice, hope, desire, trust and so on. God wasn't on the list, just a series of words. Towards the end of the conversation, I worked my way through each of these words and showed him where each of them was operating in his obsession with bodybuilding. When I was done, I said, "I think you are just as religious as me, we just have different gods." He paused for a moment and replied, "Yep. I think you're right."

Luke was a relational worshipper, and he knew it. Whilst the object of his worship wasn't God, he could clearly see he was a worshipper who was giving himself in relationship to the object of his worship. Ultimately, he was giving himself in relational worship to himself. Luke is not alone; we too are relational worshippers. We unceasingly give ourselves in relationship to people or things around us. There is always someone or something in the God slot in our lives. We love what we value most highly, and what we love most we worship.

What happened in the garden?

With the categories of relationality and worship in mind, let's revisit the fall of humanity in the Garden of Eden (Gen 3) and see if we can identify some of these threads in the actions of Adam and Eve. What was driving their eating of the fruit? Pride. Pride is a synonym for self-worship. It is when we push God out of the centre of our lives and put ourselves in his place. C.S. Lewis describes it this way: "From the moment a creature becomes aware of God as God, and itself as self, the terrible opportunity of choosing God or self as centre is opened to it."[23] Adam and Eve decided being *like* God was not enough, they wanted to *be* God. They wanted to do what they wanted, when they wanted, and how they wanted to do it. Adam and Eve's first idolatry was idolatry of the self. The creatures designed to curve away from themselves in worship and love, curved in on themselves in sinful self-love and self-worship. In doing so, they severed the moorings which kept them human, and set sail into the unknown.

In 2011, the musician Lady Gaga was interviewed by talk show host Ellen DeGeneres. In the early days of her music career, Lady Gaga was known as yet another pop star who would do and say outrageous things. But in this interview[24], she nailed down the essence of what is wrong with humanity, even as she promoted the very thing she spoke of. "Pop-culture is our religion. Through self-worship in terms of your identity, and through honouring your identity, and really fighting for who you are every single day of your life, down to your core, you can have more faith and hope in life and your future." I'm sorry Lady Gaga, that's not the solution—that's what got us into the mess in the first place. You won't fix the black hole inside of you by curving in on yourself. You just weren't made to do that.

The fall of humanity reads like a classic smash and grab. A smash and grab is a kind of robbery where thieves smash through a barrier such as a window or a door, grab as much loot as they can, and then take off. Adam and Eve smashed through the barrier God put in place (his loving direction), grabbed what they wanted (or at least what they thought they wanted), and then took off. This was the exact opposite of what they needed to do. They should have patiently waited for God and the good things He had planned for them. He had his ways and his reasons, and they could trust him. But, like a modern-day marketer, or the promoter of a buy now, pay later scheme, the serpent came along and told them they could have what they wanted and have it now—they just had to smash through the barrier and grab it. Pride and idolatry are impatient. They want what they want, and they want it now.

There is no end to the examples of humanity smashing and grabbing in the Bible. Cain, in his jealousy, didn't turn to God but murdered his brother (Gen 4). Abram and Sarai didn't wait to see how God's plan to give them a child would work out and Abram ended up having sex with his servant instead (Gen 16). Israel didn't wait for Moses to come down from Mount Sinai with God's instructions, but fashioned a golden calf to worship (Exod 32). Saul didn't wait for Samuel to come to offer the burnt sacrifice, but impatiently offered it himself (1 Sam 13). Israel couldn't wait for God and his provision, but grumbled about not having food or water in the wilderness (Exod 15–16).

Humanity continues to smash and grab, right up to this very day. Today, porn users will prefer a cheap thrill on a screen over a genuine relationship with God and a real woman, because the women they look at don't require them to do the work of a relationship. Today, humanity will self-medicate with drugs, chocolate, and coffee, rather than turn to God and wait upon the one from whom all good things flow. Today, victims will take cheap shots at those who have sinned against them because they want their justice now, rather than waiting for the vindication and justice of the Holy One, the judge of all the earth. Whenever waiting is absent, and impatience and grasping are present, you can be sure idolatry is not far away. When we don't wait for God, we mangle our relationship with him, we mangle the good plan he has in store, and we wreck the good gifts he has for us. It is no wonder the Scriptures tell us over and over to wait upon the Lord (Ps 27:14, 37:34, Isa 40:31, Hos 12:6).

Waiting, relationship and idolatry

Waiting is a relationally intensive activity. I have four sons. When they were young, I was keen to nail down some basic principles by which we would operate as a family. One of the first was the need to say sorry and ask forgiveness. I figured that a bunch of sinners living in a house would mean that hurting one another was inevitable, so saying sorry was going to need to be inevitable as well—we might as well get used to it. I also taught them they were to forgive each other. Whether the hurt was deep or shallow, they had to get there because, whether their sin was deep or shallow, Jesus forgave them.

One day, one of my boys sinned grievously against his brother. He hurt him deeply. I helped the son who had sinned to see what he had done and then brought the two boys together to sort it out. He named his sin, said sorry for doing it, and then asked his brother to forgive him. He nailed it. His brother quickly replied,

"No!" Before anyone had a chance to say anything else, the son who hurt his brother turned to me and said, "That's not right. He's supposed to forgive me!" I said to him, "Well, you hurt him deeply. He doesn't have to get there straight away. You are just going to have to wait until he does."

The idea of needing to wait for forgiveness was foreign to my son. What was he supposed to do in the meantime? The short answer was, stay in relationship with his brother as best he could, and wait until his brother was ready to forgive. Disconnecting from his sibling and staying away wouldn't help. Even though he didn't get what he wanted, what he so desperately needed (forgiveness), he needed to find a way to stay connected, to keep the door ajar, until his brother was ready to talk again. The real work of relationship happens when we aren't getting what we want from the other person. It was in this space where he (and we) needed to get to work, keeping the doubts, questions and frustration at bay until the relationship could be restored. "Why is he doing this? I want something different. Doesn't he care about me? I need to have this sorted now. What if he is planning on doing something to get back at me? This is uncomfortable." He had to wait for his brother.

Waiting is an essential part of every relationship. You can't do any relationship without needing to wait. Sometimes we mature more quickly than others, and we need to wait. Other times people get clarity and deeper revelation on something before other people do, and they need to wait. Often, we will see what is wrong in others before they see it in themselves, and we will need to wait. Most of the time others don't run on our schedule, they are either ahead of us or behind us, and we need to wait. If you want to do relationships well, then you will need to get used to waiting.

But waiting is not passive; it is the place where a lot of the hard work of relationships is done. For a time in my teaching career, I was responsible for overseeing high school detentions at lunchtime. I had a number of 'regular customers.' One, in particular, seemed strangely unaffected by the sheer volume of detentions he would receive. I asked him about it one day, "Why don't you care very much about how many detentions you get?" He said, "I have worked out how to zone out in detention. I go in and before I know it, it is over." For many of us, this is the kind of thing we imagine God is talking about when he asks us to wait. We think to wait and stop are the same thing, as though all we have to do is switch off and pretend not to care until we get what we want. In contrast, the kind of waiting God wants from us is relationally rich and oriented towards personal trust in him, rather than being connected to, and dependent upon, a certain outcome.

Most sin happens when we should be waiting. We get impatient and we fear God won't give us what we want, so we reach out and try to snatch it. In doing so, we show how the thing we want is more important to us than God. It is the very definition of idolatry. The substitution of God for some other person or thing immediately breaks our relationship with him. This dynamic can be clearly seen in the fall of humanity. In Genesis 2 and 3, God is called the 'Lord God' twenty times. This is a personal, intimate name which reflects a covenantal relationship.[25] In Genesis 3, you will notice the serpent doesn't use this title (Gen 3:1). This is not surprising. He knows God is God, but he is not in relationship with him. To him, God is powerful but distant. But as Genesis 3 progresses, to our shock, Eve follows the serpent's lead! God has become only 'God' to her, not the 'Lord God'. She was the one who was in relationship with God! Now the close one is not so close. He is still God, but he is farther away. In her impatient desire to get what she wanted, she worshipped herself and what she could get at that moment and shut down her relationship with God.

The power of idolatry is connected to the way it gives us immediacy and control, in contrast to the waiting and uncertainty of a genuine, loving relationship. Every genuine, loving relationship is an uncontrolled space. You can't control what the other person does, how they will respond to you, whether you will get what you want, and so on. Sometimes people try to control others in relationships but when they do, they mangle the relationship. It just isn't the same anymore, because the manipulation has made it about them, rather than the relationship. And even when they succeed, the love they receive from the other person does not come to them as true love, it comes to them as something they have organised, something they have worked for, and it doesn't feel like real love. It is a counterfeit. Similarly, the relationship we have with idols is a perverted one. It is more like the relationship you would have with a vending machine than a human. You put something in, and it gives you what you want. But at the core, deep down, it doesn't actually give you what you really want. It leaves you feeling hollow because you were made for something far richer and deep down you know it.

Humanity can turn anything into an idol. Indeed, the human heart is a factory of idols;[26] "Every one of us is, even from his mother's womb, expert in inventing idols."[27] While the idols of the Bible tend to fit our stereotype of what an idol is (Baal and Ashtoreth for example), idolatry can take any form. And it can sneak up on you. Like any adulterous relationship, it is an affair of the heart before it becomes an affair of the body. Physical worship is the last domino to fall. The prophet Ezekiel highlighted this when he criticised the elders of Israel for taking their idols "into their hearts" (Ezek 14:3). We have turned to the worship of idols when we love, fear, trust, obey, or desire anything more than God. Most of the time, they start out as something good—a reasonable desire such as food and water (as the Israelites experienced in the wilderness), comfort, pleasure, to name a few. But the way desire (a key New Testament idolatry category[28]) works is it battles for control of our hearts (Jas 4:1–4) and, once it has control, it becomes the god we worship, serve, love, and hope in. When we worship sexual pleasure, we treat others like objects and end up in adultery, or have multiple sexual partners, or develop an addiction to pornography.

When we worship the opinions of others, we end up doing things we don't really want to do, or lying about what we think, or we become obsessively anxious about the way we appear. When we worship comfort, we end up pursuing it in self-destructive ways such as drugs or binge-eating; sometimes we pursue it in ways which make others' lives very uncomfortable. We want what we want, and idols are the servants who get it for us.

Need and idolatry

But idolatry isn't only a high-handed grasping for something that is not ours; it is also what we reach for in our needy, disconnected state. When humanity relationally disconnected from God, everything went haywire. We quickly found out that we didn't have what it takes to sit in God's seat. While God is infinite, self-sufficient, and self-contained, we are finite and dependent. God doesn't need anyone or anything (Acts 17:25), he is in control (Jer 32:27), and he does whatever pleases him (Ps 115:3). If you put a human in a sealed room and gave them nothing, they would die. If you could do the same to God, he would happily live forever. We are finite and needy by design. He made us to need him, to need each other, to need sleep, to need wisdom from outside ourselves ... and so much more.

When we turned in on ourselves in self-worship, we severed our connection to the one who provided everything we needed to be truly us and our 'need' exploded. God was the one who consistently loved us—his power and love helped us to be secure in a world outside of our control. Our identity was connected to him; he was the one who gave us ultimate purpose and meaning. He was our greatest pleasure, the one from whom all lesser pleasures are a mere shadow. He provided wisdom and help; in him was life itself (John 1:4). And in a moment all those life-giving connections disappeared, like an astronaut deliberately disconnecting their air supply on a spacewalk.

We have always been needy.[29] Our neediness was there before sin. But now it is worse, much worse. Now we have to carry the ravages of sin and corruption on top of our baseline neediness. What are we to do? We just don't have what it takes to make our lives go.

In our separation from God, we quickly realise we need help from outside of ourselves to make our lives go. Logic would tell us we should return to God but, instead of returning to God, humanity has opted for gathering or creating idols which serve our self-worshipping ends. And there is no end to the number of idols offering to take God's place. In the book of Isaiah, there is a powerful satirical piece on the stupidity of idolatry. The prophet describes an idol maker and worshipper, from his crafting of the idol to the worship of it. The man chops a tree down, selects the wood, and carefully shapes the idol. Then at the end, he bows down and worships the object he made saying, "Deliver me, for you are my god!" (Isa 44:17) Can you see what is happening here? The idol worshipper has created something to do what he can't do for himself—offer deliverance or rescue. He knows his limits; he is not self-contained, he is needy by nature, so he employs the service of an idol to help look after him. This is another underlying reason behind idolatry—we don't have everything we need so we reach out and gather the idols we think will help us. But these idols, rather than assisting us, only enslave us further, robbing us of whatever humanity we had left. We are in quite a spot of bother.

A jilted lover

Much to our surprise, we find throughout the pages of the Old Testament that God is not done with humanity. It turns out this intensely personal and relational God is determined to have a relationship with us. While he could have killed us all in an instant, or withdrawn and become merely a judge or a distant king, or even become the uninvolved god of the deists, he didn't. He is after much more. He wants a loving, committed, exclusive relationship with us—he wants our hearts.

But there is a problem. The people God created to be in relationship with him are unfaithful. We are "twisted like a deceitful bow" (Ps 78:57). Even God's best people have had moments of major failure, and we are no different. While we have moments of faithfulness to God, we also go astray in our hearts (Heb 3:10). It isn't that a better deal comes along or that we just want to check out another business option, it is about our hearts. Every time we blow it, every time we turn from him, we go astray in our hearts and give ourselves away to another lover. Adam and Eve didn't just disobey God, they went astray in their hearts. The fall happened before they ate the fruit. They preferred the words of a serpent to those of the one true God. They preferred themselves to God.

Our unfaithfulness to God matters to him. But it doesn't matter the way we sometimes think it does. This misunderstanding may be part of the reason Adam and Eve opted to hide rather than confess. We expect God to come at us like a vengeful judge, hell-bent on exacting judgement and justice, or as a fiery king determined to put down a rebellion. But he doesn't do either. To our great surprise, he comes as a jilted lover. A sovereign jilted lover, but a jilted lover nonetheless. We rejected him and cast him aside without so much as a thought and it hits him to the core, to his very heart. And he lets us know.

God reserves some of the bluntest language for his people who have been unfaithful to him. It isn't legal or accounting language, it is richly relational language, it is marital language. Here is a small sample:

> ... the LORD said to Hosea, "Go, take to yourself a wife of whoredom and have children of whoredom, for the land commits great whoredom by forsaking the LORD." (Hos 1:2)

> Yet she increased her whoring, remembering the days of her youth, when she played the whore in the land of Egypt and lusted after her lovers there ... (Ezek 23:19–20)

> With their idols they have committed adultery ... (Ezek 23:37)

> "Have you seen what she did, that faithless one, Israel, how she went up on every high hill and under every green tree, and there played the whore? And I thought, 'After she has done all this she will return to me,' but she did not return ..." (Jer 3:6–7)

Do you find this language jarring? This small selection only scratches the surface of what can be found in Scripture. It is common for God to speak this way about the relationship he has with his people. All sin is relational at its core. It's not just a random thing you do, or a small thing for a brief moment, or something you couldn't help. It is personal, deeply personal. You embraced other gods right in front of his face (an alternative translation of the first commandment in Exodus 20:3). Our offence is much worse than we thought.[30] He was faithful and committed, we were not, and he feels the sting of our betrayal.

Be careful, though, that you don't misunderstand the nature of the hurt God feels. He is not hurt by our unfaithfulness because he is needy, as though he were insecure and needed you to love him to feel okay about himself.[31] He doesn't need you, remember? The reason he is hurt by your unfaithfulness is because he loves you. If he didn't love you, it wouldn't bother him like that. But he does love you and, in loving you, he puts himself in a position to be hurt by you. "To love at all is to be vulnerable. Love anything and your heart will certainly be wrung and possibly be broken."[32] The one to whom we have been unfaithful, the one whose heart we have broken, is not a dog or cat or even another human. It is God himself.

What have we done?

Saying sorry

As a counsellor and pastor, I sometimes get the opportunity to guide spouses through the reconciliation process in the aftermath of an affair. I have seen how important healthy steps of reconciliation are in the early stages of this process. In this period, actions and reactions are analysed so closely it can be hard for the relationship to breathe. While both spouses need to move towards each other to rebuild the relationship, the weight of responsibility is not evenly balanced. Most of the relational work must be done by the person sinned against, not the unfaithful spouse. But this doesn't mean there is no work for the unfaithful spouse to do. If they don't turn up with some robust confession and repentance, then the chances of the relationship being restored are slim at best. This is true of our relationship with God too. The way we turn up after committing spiritual adultery will be critical to the restoration of our relationship with God.

One of the most confronting passages of Scripture on idolatry and repentance, is found in the book of James. Throughout his letter, James has been emphasising how desires can get too big, get control of our hearts, and lead to entrenched combative conflict (Jas 4:1–3). Whilst James is referring to a specific application of the principle, it is relevant to every other sin also. Immediately after this short but powerful description of the intersection between our desires and our hearts, James punches us right in the nose, "You adulterous people!" (Jas 4:4) The people he was writing to weren't just arguing, they were committing spiritual adultery. Their sin was relational by nature, not because they were arguing with others, but because in their hearts they loved the things they wanted more than God. After his rebuke, James moves on to teach the people how to say sorry. In essence, he answers the question, "How do you turn up after you have been unfaithful to God?" He begins and ends with humility and in the middle gives four key principles of repentance.

James assures his readers that there is more grace from God for them, but they will only get it if they are humble. "But he gives more grace. Therefore it says, 'God opposes the proud but gives grace to the humble'" (Jas 4:6). Any adulterer wanting reconciliation is going to need more grace, that is a given. But the only way to get it is if they show up humbly. They need to get themselves out of the centre and turn up needy. Easier said than done!

Pride can easily sneak into our repentance. It is about self-protection and self-sufficiency. Pride says *I don't need your help, I am good on my own*. It never leads to reconciliation, only competition and division.[33] Here are three examples of repentance where pride puts self in the centre:

1. Selective confessions for the sake of self-protection. Don't tell the bad bits. Only tell the bits which you need to. No need to get into more trouble than you have to.

2. Defend yourself while you are confessing. Tell them all about the mitigating circumstances because most of it wasn't your fault. Surround your sorry with explanations. You wouldn't have done it, at least not as badly, if those things hadn't happened.

3. You couldn't handle the guilt anymore. We confess to get clean because we don't like feeling dirty. But then we go right back and repeat what got us dirty in the first place.

Pride doesn't attract grace because it doesn't need it. Humility, on the other hand, is about a low posture of heart and an openness about one's need of help. In repentance, it puts the other person in the centre and has their best interests at heart. God loves the humble. Humility attracts his grace like iron filings to a magnet. Humility stirs up God's heart to be gracious and prepares our hearts to receive his grace.

The first component of saying sorry that James outlines is submission to God and resistance to Satan. "Submit yourselves therefore to God. Resist the devil, and he will flee from you" (Jas 4:7). This is a rewinding of what we saw in the garden. In the fall, Adam and Eve stopped submitting to God and in doing so, failed to resist the devil. The devil's objective is division between God and his people. He does this by luring them out of submission to God and towards self-determination. In his temptation, Satan tells us submission to God is suffocating and self-determination is liberating, when it is actually the opposite. Instead of liberation and life, Adam and Eve ended up in slavery and death.

It's always the way self-determination will end, because it is only in submission to God that we find life. Imagine a fishbowl on your benchtop with a goldfish in it. One day this fish gets to thinking the fishbowl is too limiting for it, so it takes a deep breath, swims really hard and jumps out of the bowl onto the bench. As it does you can hear it crying out, "I'm free!" But is it free? Is it liberated? Hardly. It is more enslaved than ever because it is not submitting to its need to be in the water. Submission to God says to him, "I will do what you say, I will listen to you, you are the authoritative one in my life, you know what's best."

The second component of saying sorry is the need to draw near. "Draw near to God, and he will draw near to you" (Jas 4:8). If you have been unfaithful, draw near to the one you have hurt. You can't reconcile with someone you don't like, but if you do like that person and you are sorry for what you did, then drawing near makes all kinds of sense. How do you draw near to God? The same way you do in any other relationship. You take an interest in what he likes, you listen to him, you care about what matters to him, you treasure him and care about him. You find ways to know and be known by him, and you do what you can to be in his presence. Now don't get bogged down by who draws near first. I don't think James is trying to make any particular point on this. He is simply saying if you have been unfaithful, draw near to God. After all, there is no such thing as a healthy relationship where one person is passive. Both people need to be active. And be assured, if you draw near, he won't leave you hanging and he won't give you the cold shoulder. He will come close.

The third component of saying sorry involves the need to cut off contact with your illicit lovers. You need to stop the affair. "Cleanse your hands, you sinners, and purify your hearts, you double-minded" (Jas 4:8). When you turn up, make sure you come with clean hands (or actions) and a clean heart (or motivations). To not do this would be like trying to reconcile with your spouse after an affair while continuing to communicate with your illicit lover via text message. Be careful you don't romanticise the sin even as you are confessing it. If we really want to return to God, then we will need to smash our idols, sometimes literally. We simply can't keep flirting with our lovers if we want things to be right with God.

The final component of saying sorry is demonstrating appropriate sorrow for what we have done. "Be wretched and mourn and weep. Let your laughter be turned to mourning and your joy to gloom" (Jas 4:9). Ecclesiastes 3:4 tells us there is a time to laugh and a time to cry—but don't get them the wrong way around. What you have done is grievous and hurtful. Laughing, silliness, or being carefree doesn't match what you have done, mourning does. If what you have done is bad, be sad and cry about it, literally. Have you ever cried about your sin when repenting to God? How long ago was it?

Exaltation

Picture this. It is the moment you have been dreading. You ran off and had an affair with another lover. You regret it so much now and wish it never happened. But it did, and you can't take it back. You have made the necessary preparations. You have your apology all sorted out and it is time for the first reconciliation meeting. God is waiting for you in the next room. It is time to go and confess what you have done to him. You know as soon as you walk through the door that you will be met by a righteousness, holiness and light that words cannot express. And you, you are covered in guilt, shame, and filth. You have nothing to offer him and you know it. You take your time to rehearse over and over your "I'm sorry" speech. You know it won't be enough, nothing will ever be enough, but it is all you have to offer. You don't even feel worthy enough to walk through the doorway. Slithering on the floor probably suits you better. That is who you have become. You decide grovelling is the way to go so you get down on your knees. You reach up to the doorknob, turn it and begin crawling in, being careful not to look

God in the eye. You can't bear the thought of locking eyes with him. To even have him look at you is too much. You begin begging, "I am so sorry. I blew it. I cheated on you. I got it so wrong. Can you ever forgive me?"

At this point, you have done almost everything you can. There is nothing more you can do, nothing more you can say to make things right. It actually feels worse in the moment, because now the mess is public, it is in plain sight. You repeat your sorry over and over, hoping the repetition will in some way make you more deserving. But this only serves to highlight, in no uncertain terms, the powerlessness you feel. Because now it is over to him. The lion's share of the relational work has now shifted from you to him, from the offender to the offended. If he doesn't love you anymore, it's over. If he doesn't have any more grace, it's over. If he doesn't have any more forgiveness for you, it's over. Your destiny hangs in the balance. The ball is in his court. No one controls him. No one tells him what to do. It all comes down to his heart. What will he do?

Much to your surprise, he interrupts you and, like a cold drink on a sweltering day, soothes you with the most beautiful words.

"I still love you. I forgive you."

You are stunned. "What? Really?"

He takes your filthy clothes from you, dresses you in pure clean clothes (Zech 3:3–4) and says, "Come up here and sit with me."

He gives more grace ... Humble yourselves before the Lord, and he will exalt you. (Jas 4:6,10)

Scripture reading
Romans 1

For reflection and discussion

1. What do you think is wrong with you? What personal problems leave you feeling clueless?

2. Who or what typically becomes the object of your relational worship when it isn't God?

3. Where can you observe self-worship in your life? Where do you love yourself more than you love God?

4. When have you 'smashed and grabbed' to get what you want? What effect did it have? Who normally bears the cost of your smashing and grabbing?

5. Most sin happens when we should be waiting. We get impatient and we fear God won't give us what we want, so we reach out and try to snatch it. Where do you get impatient? How is it connected to your relational worship?

6. Where do your idols leave you feeling hollow? What needs open up in your life when you disconnect from God? Be as specific as possible.

7. Pride can sneak into our repentance in at least three ways:
   a. We can be selective in our confessions in an effort to protect ourselves
   b. We can be defensive and self-justifying in the midst of confessing our wrongdoing
   c. We confess only to rid ourselves of the weight of our guilt

   Where has pride snuck into your repentance to God or others?

8. There are four key components to relational reconciliation with God:
   a. Submitting to him
   b. Drawing near to him
   c. Cutting off contact with your illicit lovers (smashing your idols)
   d. Feeling appropriate sorrow for your sin

   Which one do you find the hardest?

4. The shape of dehumanisation

In *The Lord of the Rings*, J.R.R. Tolkien tells the story of two hobbits called Sméagol and Déagol. They were relatives and friends. One day, when they were out fishing, Déagol hooked a particularly large fish. It was so big and strong it pulled him out of the boat and into the water. He held his rod tight as the fish dragged him down toward the bottom of the river. When he eventually opened his eyes, he saw a gold ring on the riverbed. Unbeknownst to him, it wasn't just any ring, it was *the* ring which made the wearer invisible and gave them great power. It had been lost for some time and he, by chance, had found it. Déagol quickly let go of the rod, scooped up the ring, and crawled out onto the riverbank. Shortly after, Sméagol saw the ring Déagol had in his hand and became obsessed with having it. But Déagol didn't want to give it to him and a scuffle broke out over the ring. Neither hobbit was prepared to give way. The conflict escalated until Sméagol choked his friend to death to get the ring. A horrific scene.

While Sméagol was obsessed with what the ring could do *for* him, he didn't bargain on what it would do *to* him. The ring was to have a powerfully caustic effect on who he was. It was a death by a thousand cuts. Slowly but surely Sméagol became more physically decrepit and more mentally deranged. He ended up a shadow of his former self, destined to live alone in the mountains, eating raw fish caught with his invisible fingers.[34] No longer was he called Sméagol. Gollum was his new name, derived from the gurgling sound he made in his throat.[35]

The ring gave him power, but it also destroyed him, and he ended up in a love/hate relationship with it. He loved the power it gave to him, but he hated the effect it had on him. Gandalf, the white wizard, described Gollum's relationship with the ring well: "He hated it and loved it, as he hated and loved himself. He could not get rid of it. He had no will left in the matter."[36] While he had chosen it in the beginning he had lost all choice in the end—he had become a slave, a pawn of the ring.

The film adaptation of *The Lord of the Rings* vividly depicts the devolution of Sméagol into Gollum through a progression of scenes which culminate with him crawling through a mountain cave alone. As he does, we hear him saying, "And we wept precious, we wept, we so alone ... And we forgot the taste of bread, the sound of trees. The softness of the wind. We even forgot our own name. My precious."[37] The de-hobbiting of Sméagol was complete. He had almost completely lost touch with who he was. Eventually, he lost the ring and embarked on a long quest to get it back, alongside others in the story who were on a quest to destroy it. In the end, his efforts to regain the ring led to the final unwinding of who he was—death itself.

What we love and who we become

The connection between what we love and who we become is a well-known human phenomenon. You only need to have a quick glance through the movies we watch and the stories we read to see this plotline popping up all over the place. From Narcissus of the ancient Greeks, who fell in love with his own reflection; to Ebenezer Scrooge and his feathered Disney namesake Scrooge McDuck, a stingy, wealthy, cranky person; to Sméagol. Like it or not, there is a direct connection between what you love and who you are. Whilst fictional stories of this sort abound, real-life stories abound too. From the worship of pleasure and the drugs which deliver it, to the love of justice gone wrong and the revenge which accompanies it, to the love of comfort and the anger so often attached to it. What you love changes you, for good or for ill. Give yourself to God in relational worship and you will progressively become more human; turn from him to false gods and dehumanisation is what you can expect.

Sometimes it appears that idols 'work' for people. But they never really do; they always have a dehumanising effect on their worshippers. Idols always change you, and never for the better. The connection between your loves and your identity was hardwired into humanity from the very beginning. In Genesis, we learn God made humanity to be a kind of mirror, to image and reflect his glory and goodness. But in our rebellion, humanity turned from God and, as mirrors, we continued to image the object of our affections. We didn't stop reflecting, we just stopped reflecting God and began imaging things of far less value. As G.K. Beale puts it, we became what we worshipped.[38] Whatever we revere, we "resemble, either for ruin or restoration."[39]

The relational worship of God is critical because of the way it anchors us to the one who keeps us truly human, the one who makes us who we are. It doesn't tell us everything we need to know about humanity, but it does tell us about the most important bit, the engine room of proper human functioning. If our relational worship of God is central to who we are, then we can expect any break in it to have a devastating effect on the way we operate. Unsurprisingly, this is exactly what we find. The disordering of our relational worship disorders humanity in five key areas: disordered loves, disordered dominion, disordered reality, disordered relationality, and disordered relationships.

Disordered

Disordered loves

This may be a strange way to put it, but the love of God is the apex predator in our lives. The apex predator in nature is the animal at the top of the food chain, such as a lion, an orca, or a crocodile. They keep everything down the line in place and in order. Scientists are aware of this dynamic and regularly warn others about how things can get out of whack when the apex predator is taken away; animals end up doing things that they normally wouldn't do, leading to other negative knock-on effects in the ecosystem. The love of God is also like this. It is *the* love which keeps all our other loves in order. When you stop loving God the most, all your other loves get out of whack. You end up loving other things too much or not enough; you end up loving what you shouldn't and not loving what you should.[40] We are lovers by design, but that design is structured with God's love at the top. When our love for God is not the strongest love, the other loves in our lives become scattered and disordered.

In its day, one of the more shocking examples of disordered love was disclosed in a widely reported interview with musician John Mayer.[41] In the interview, Mayer explained his views on pornography and sex, and how he preferred to be at home with pornography than be with a real person. "I'm more comfortable in my imagination than I am in actual human discovery. The best days of my life are when I've dreamed about a sexual encounter with someone I've already been with."[42] Mayer admitted to preferring the cheap thrill of porn in preference to doing the real work of a loving relationship. The title of an article about the interview, "Self Love", aptly summarises many of Mayer's comments. You are not meant to love yourself more than others, John, and you are not meant to love a counterfeit more than a real woman—women are not a means to your own ends. Your loves are disordered.

Unfortunately, stories of high-level disordered loves abound.

Just take a quick scroll through today's news. You will find stories of people loving power more than compassion, others who love money more than people, and those who love sexual pleasure more than the people they take it from. It's a mess. But before you get too comfortable, it isn't just them. It isn't just those people out there. The disordering of loves has trickled down into the details of our lives too. We are the ones who react angrily to our children interrupting our 'me time' for some help with their homework. We are the ones who treat our pets better than our own children. We are the ones who prefer our own comfort, rather than helping someone in need. Once you find the first disordered love you will begin to see them everywhere.

Disordered dominion

Exercising dominion is a key part of who God is and who we are. In the opening chapter of Scripture, God exercised his dominion over a world which was formless and void (Gen 1:2), bringing about life and goodness. "And God said … and it was so … and God saw that it was good" (Gen 1:20–21). At the end of the chapter, God created humanity, male and female, and commanded them to exercise dominion over creation in a way similar to the way God himself did. They were mandated to bring about order and goodness, under his rule and authority. And they did for a time—until the fall, when dominion went haywire.

Dominion and worship are connected—whatever you worship, you serve. In the beginning, God created us to worship him, serve him, and have dominion over creation. But in the fall, humanity turned their worship away from the creator to creation, and God's created order was tipped upside down. Paul teaches us about this dynamic in Romans: "They exchanged the truth about God for a lie and worshiped and served the creature rather than the Creator" (Rom 1:25). This is the exact inversion of the creation mandate to exercise dominion (Gen 1:26,28). Instead of worshipping God, serving him and having dominion over creation, humanity worshipped creation, served creation, and creation had dominion over them—and it continues to today. When worship gets perverted, dominion gets inverted. This is how it works: worship and serve God and you will have dominion over creation; worship and serve creation, and it will have dominion over you.

Dominion and identity are also connected. God has designed for there to be a direct link between the exercise of dominion and your identity. To put it another way, God has designed for there to be a direct link between your dominion and your dignity, or how human you feel. Exercise dominion over creation for good, as God did in the first chapter of Genesis, and it will feed into your sense of personal value—you will take your place in creation under God and it will feel right. There's dignity in it. Worship creation, and it will have dominion over you, and you will feel that too. The value you feel is connected to the object of your worship. Worship God and you will be filled with value; worship creation, and you will struggle with your value. Worship your phone and what it can give you and you have just placed a cap on your value. Worship chocolate or food and you can never be more valuable than chocolate or food. Worship something worthless and you become worthless: "they ... went after worthlessness, and became worthless" (Jer 2:5). Don't be surprised if you feel devalued and less than human when you are worshipping something other than God—that is just the way it works.

I like to exercise dominion over my lawn by mowing it. While it often takes hard work and normally generates some sweat, at the end I feel satisfied because I have brought order and goodness to my patch of grass. The parts which were too long or out of control have been brought back into line. I hardly ever tell anyone about the satisfaction I feel, but I do enjoy the order and goodness it brings. It feels weird to admit it, but when I mow it says something about me and my place in the world—my grass doesn't rule me, I rule it. I am of more significance and value than my grass. You may not mow the lawn, but you might do other things which bring about order and goodness. Some people name species, or bring order to financial accounts, or remove cancers, or clean teenagers' rooms. There are lots of ways to exercise dominion over creation and, every time we do, it says something about who we are.

While we have been made to serve what we worship, the nature of our service of idols is vastly different to the service of the living God. When we give ourselves to God in relational worship, we become free-er and more truly human, but when we give ourselves to idols we end up in suffocating, dehumanising slavery. While you won't find the word addiction in the Bible, you will find the term slavery. Slavery is the biblical category for addiction. Slavery (addiction) is an entrenched worship disorder. While it feels like we are choosing the idol in the beginning, we end up out of control and feeling like it is the idol that is choosing us. We get stuck and feel powerless, as though it has some kind of spell on us. This descent into powerlessness can develop quickly or slowly. It can be the result of a physical dependency, such as alcohol or drugs, a mental dependency generated by our habits (such as the well-documented effects of pornography on the brains of those who view it regularly), or can simply be a long-term functional saviour we have become dependent on. Whatever shape addiction takes, Welch's term "voluntary slavery"[43] labels it well.

Disordered reality

The worship of idols always leaves you living in a false reality. Why? Because the essence of idolatry is the exchanging of "the truth about God for a lie" (Rom 1:25). Lies are false realities masquerading as the truth, and idols are lies. They are 'no-gods' pretending to be God, and 'no-things' pretending to be something other than what they really are. Whilst the Old Testament at times addresses them as real, it goes to great lengths to emphasise they are dead, inanimate blocks of wood (Isa 44:19, Ps 115:4–7, Jer 10:5). But the moment you believe an idol will give you what you want or save you, it comes alive and you begin believing things which are not true. In some ways, it is like a Hollywood movie. Our trust in the idol has the effect of bringing it to life, even if it is only in our imagination, and it seems bigger, better, and more caring than before. This is one reason your family and friends don't understand your idols like you do. They haven't put their personal trust in that same idol and animated it like you have. The magic just isn't there for them. But the truth is idols can't breathe or move, they don't care about you, they aren't loving, and they can't save you. Your phone is just minerals, chemicals, electricity and algorithms. Money is plastic, paper and pixels on a screen. Idols aren't anyone, they aren't personal, they are only things.

Idols always lie to you. And the biggest lie is the one about them being God. They aren't God, but they tell you they are, and once you have let in the first lie, the rest swarm in behind it. They tell you they are powerful and can give you what you want, when in reality they use their power to enslave you. They tell you true life will be found in having them, when in reality your life will ebb away, bit by bit. They tell you they will save you when, in reality, they will only get you into more trouble. They lie to you about what is good and evil[44] and they never deliver on their promises. You can't trust them.

When you put your trust in an idol, you don't just get the idol, you get the idol's whole system with it. Like a bunch of unwanted groupies, idols bring with them their own moral framework, unique guilt and shame, and an alternative system of atonement. To illustrate, consider the idol of living for the approval of others. If you worship this idol, then your moral code, or the framework you use to decide what is good or bad, will be connected to what other people think. So far so good. Well, kind of good, because it gets complicated. What other people think varies from person to person, group to group, and day to day. Some will want you to be funny and the life of the party, others will want you to be quiet and reserved, some will like your family background, others won't want you to talk about it. It's a floating, ever-changing moral system; good luck trying to know what it is from one moment to the next, let alone living within it. Unfortunately, knowing when you have broken the rules is easier to identify than the rules themselves—an awkward silence or a terse response will convict you. Then the guilt and shame will hit you along with the need to get busy working your way back to being a good person again—enter self-atonement. This could come in the form of repetitive public self-condemnation (if you condemn your badness enough then you must be a good person), or it could be an extra dash of extroversion/life-of-the-party as you work the crowd in an effort to win them back. But even if you make it back to being a good person in this system, the sad reality is you will inevitably get something wrong and the whole cycle will repeat. It's like an out of control treadmill which you can't get off. You run harder and harder, yet you never seem to get anywhere. Whilst in the moment this idol's system seems real, it's a sham. It doesn't exist. It's not even a thing. To live your life constantly fearing other people's opinions is to live life in an alternate reality. The only law which matters is God's, the only true guilt and shame are connected to his law, and the only way out is the grace and love of a saviour who died in your place to cleanse and cover you.

    I saw one of the starkest examples of an idol and its false system in one of my high school classes several years ago. I was busy teaching when I noticed a student hitting herself on the leg with a plastic ruler. While I didn't pay too much attention to it the first time around, she kept doing it in my class, lesson after lesson. I knew a few things about her; she wasn't one of the 'cool' kids, she didn't have any 'cool' friends, and she didn't have the 'right' body shape. I wondered whether any of these things were connected to what she was doing. Eventually, I had seen enough and at the end of one of my classes, I asked her why she was constantly hitting herself on the leg. She told me she was a bad person and she was hitting herself on the leg to punish herself for being a bad person. It broke my heart. Imagine being stuck in that false reality. Her idol was acceptance by her peers. There was a moral law she had broken by virtue of who she was, she felt the guilt and shame associated with it, and she was engaged in self-atonement. Her entire system was a lie. None of it was even real. The way she looked didn't make her good or bad, the guilt and shame she felt were based on a faulty moral law, and the self-atonement she employed was never going to make her a good person. She was working hard, she was tired, and she wasn't going anywhere.

Getting out of idolatry is always harder than getting into it. This is because deception always seems so real, so true, even though it is a false reality (not to mention other cultural and biological factors which also play their part). You think you are right and everyone else is wrong. You doggedly think you are the only one who has a correct read on the situation, even when no one else agrees with you. You think you are the only one living in the true reality when, in actuality, you are the one living in a false reality. In the end, your life will become so disordered and disoriented you will wind up like the idol maker/worshipper in Isaiah 44:20: "a deluded heart has led him astray, and he cannot deliver himself or say, 'Is there not a lie in my right hand?'"

Idols. Deceive. You.

Disordered relationality

The worship of idols also makes people less personal and relational. It shuts them down to others. Some time ago, I was on the phone with a friend of mine who works for a Christian organisation helping people with financial problems. We were talking about the effects of idolatry and addiction. He made this profound comment, "I think the opposite of addiction is relationship", and then moved on to his next thought, but it stopped me in my tracks. He was so right. When people turn to idols, they switch off relationally—they become less personal. Some of you know what I am talking about. You have experienced this with friends or family. They can be so warm and relational only to suddenly switch off when they are in pursuit of their idol. They are physically still there, and you might get the odd groan or single syllable word, but they are distracted and have given their attention to something else. All you are left with is a cardboard cut-out. Perhaps you have even asked them, "where are you?" This dynamic can be seen in Psalm 115:

> Their idols are silver and gold, the work of human hands. They have mouths, but do not speak; eyes, but do not see. They have ears, but do not hear; noses, but do not smell. They have hands, but do not feel; feet, but do not walk; and they do not make a sound in their throat. Those who make them become like them; so do all who trust in them. (Ps 115:4–8)

In this passage, the psalmist contrasts God and idols. God is a person and is intensely personal. He can choose, speak, and act intentionally.[45] He is the living God (a biblical term that captures the essence of God's personhood).[46] He can move towards us in relationship and we can move towards him. Idols, on the other hand, are dead—they are neither persons nor personal. The more that idol worshippers worship dead, non-personal idols, the more they become like them—less personal and less relational.

The worship of idols is a perversion of the way God has designed us to operate. While the relationship God seeks to have with us is close and personal, one akin to family, the relationship we have with idols is more like a vending machine. We control it, we provide what the idol wants, and we get what we need. It isn't normal. It isn't a real relationship. Idols allow access to a god without God, and transformation without relationship.[47] Or, in other words, you get a god, but they aren't God, and you get changed, but in a non-relational way. Eugene Peterson captures this beautifully:

> An idol is god with all the God taken out. God depersonalized, God derelationalized, a god that we can use and enlist and fantasize without ever once having to (maybe "getting to" is the better phrase) receive

or give love, and then go on to live, however falteringly, at our most human. The essence of idolatry is depersonalization. The idol is a form of divinity that requires no personal relationship. The idol is a form of divinity that I can manipulate and control.[48]

Disordered relationships

The giving of yourself relationally to idols not only has an effect on you, it also has a massive effect on those around you. One of the classic arguments of those who want to do as they please is 'it's not hurting anybody'. But when you are a relational creature, made to love and be loved, know and be known, there is no such thing as a victimless sin. Give yourself to an idol and you will actively sin against others and deprive them of the good God would have you do for them (Jas 4:17). In the words of Harold Best, "self-worship ... cannot be contained. In its perversity it infects those who come near its self-worshiping centre."[49]

Idolatry doesn't just depersonalise you; it depersonalises the people with whom you are in relationship. James masterfully unpacks the way this works:

> What causes quarrels and what causes fights among you? Is it not this, that your passions are at war within you? You desire and do not have, so you murder. You covet and cannot obtain, so you fight and quarrel. You do not have, because you do not ask. You ask and do not receive, because you ask wrongly, to spend it on your passions. (Jas 4:1–3)

Most trouble begins with a good desire which has become too large, inordinate. This is the origin of most idolatry. Idolatry isn't mainly a problem with desire, it is a problem with the size of the desire.[50] Once a desire for something good has become too big and taken control of you, the next inevitable step is the sense that you have to have it. Once you have decided you have to have it, then you will begin to expect that those who love you will help you to get it.[51]

But before I go on, stop for a moment and notice a subtle demotion you have given to those around you. No longer are they glorious imagers of God created to serve him, they are now your servants and are tasked with getting you what you want. Sometimes these people make it clear they don't want to be your servants. Perhaps you have caught yourself at this point thinking, "If only they helped me to get what I want, then everything would be okay." But they don't, and you slide down further toward major conflict. In an effort to stop the progression and get what we want, we can turn to manipulation or control, but that doesn't work either because those around you are also serving idols. It turns out they want what they want and aren't willing to give it up to give us what we want. So we kindly paraphrase the following, "If you won't help me get what I want, then get out of my way." But then they don't! Now the problem is even bigger. Now you don't just have one person committed to their idol, you have two, and the people and their idols are at odds with one another. What comes next? Conflict. Big-time conflict. And this is where it can get really messy. If they stay in your way for long enough, and you are determined enough to get what you want, you will end up killing for it, metaphorically or literally. Like Sméagol, murder is the natural endpoint for those who are doggedly determined to get what they want (Jas 4:2). Remember how we got here? Your desires got too big, and other people were reduced to objects so you could get what you wanted. You depersonalised and dehumanised them.

Take a quick look around and you will see countless examples of relationships which have been disordered by idolatry. When we worship sex, for example, it turns other people into objects for our sexual satisfaction. We don't care about them and we have no interest in doing the work of a real relationship. Once we are done with them, we push them aside and move on to the next person (2 Sam 13:15). For some of us, idolatry changes the way we see our children—they morph from magnificent creations of God to obstacles stopping us from getting what we want, so we overreact, get angry, and swat them out of the way like pesky flies. Sometimes people are a means to our ends. We want them to think well of us so we flatter them, saying things about them which are exaggerated, in the hope they will like us. But in the end, it isn't about them. It was never about them; it is about us.

Disordered loves, disordered dominion, disordered reality, disordered relationality, and disordered relationships. We have become eyesores. Our false loves and the gods we worship have disfigured us. Sure, we might look okay on the outside, but we are not even close to what God originally intended. Can you see it? Do you feel it? Like cellar-dwellers, we prefer darkness to light (John 3:19), we glory in our shame (Phil 3:19), we love what kills us (1 Pet 2:11), we invent ways of doing evil (Rom 1:30), and we dehumanise each other (Gal 5:15). Although there is some residual humanity left in us (Gen 9:6), 'the fall of humanity' is an apt description for our situation. We have fallen a long way from where we were.

Who will love us?

The situation we find ourselves in bears many of the hallmarks of the classic fairy tale *Beauty and the Beast*. Disney's adaptation[52] opens with the story of a young prince who lived in an amazing castle. While he was handsome on the outside, he was spoiled, selfish and ugly on the inside. One night an old woman came to his castle and requested shelter from the cold. He was repulsed by her and turned her away. She turned out to be an enchantress who, in response to his lack of love, put a curse on the prince. She turned him into a hideous beast and told him the curse would remain on him until "he could learn to love and be loved in return."[53] The prince became on the outside what he was on the inside.

Like any good story, *Beauty and the Beast* resonates with us because it isn't just about Beauty and the Beast, it is about us too. The closer we look at the prince/beast, the more he looks like us. The prince lived the contradiction of being handsome on the outside, yet ugly on the inside. We live the contradiction of being made in the image of God, yet living out of the disfigurement of sin. We know what it is like to be glorious, yet ugly. We have been ravaged by our false loves, and there isn't much good left. Like the prince, we know that love, the thing we need most, is the thing we least deserve. And we cry out alongside the disfigured prince, "Who could love a beast?"

There is a true story in the Bible which bears many of the aspects of *Beauty and the Beast*, but it is even better, because the ugliness is uglier, and the love is infinitely sweeter. It is the story of Hosea the prophet. Hosea prophesied in the 8th century BC, before the fall and exile of the northern kingdom of Israel and the southern kingdom of Judah.[54] The book of Hosea clues us into its purpose early on. God commands Hosea to, "Go, take to yourself a wife of whoredom and have children of whoredom, for the land commits great whoredom by forsaking the LORD" (Hos 1:2). Hosea was to love and marry Gomer, a woman with a wandering, ugly heart.

Our typical romantic comedy understanding of love expects Hosea, a good man, to tame the wild sexual flings of his wife. She just needs a good man, someone who will love her for who she is. Once she has that, she will change. That is the way love stories are supposed to go. But this one is different. Hosea's faithful love didn't change Gomer's heart. It continued to be wayward in the worst possible way—she was a prostitute. Her infidelity wasn't about love; it was about money. She didn't love the other men at all. She sold herself to them for sex. It was all a selfish ruse.

As we work our way through the book, we discover Hosea doing the unthinkable. He goes to the marketplace and buys his wife (Hos 3:2)! He had to pay money to get her back. This is love on a far grander scale than we are accustomed to. Eugene Peterson exposes our famished understanding of love in his introduction to the book of Hosea in The Message, "We live in a world awash in love stories. Most of them are lies. They are not love stories at all—they are lust stories, sex-fantasy stories, domination stories. From the cradle we are fed on lies about love."[55] But this story is about love, true love; not the love of Hosea for Gomer, but the love of God for his people. Our wonder at how Hosea could love Gomer is meant to give way to our wondering how God could love his adulterous people, how he could love us.

The unfaithfulness of God's people made them ugly, beastly. They became easily deceived and senseless (7:11), they spoke lies about God (7:13), they were driven by self-interest (2:5), they carried an adulterous look on their face (2:2), they committed adultery in their marriage bed (8:11) and they had within them a spirit of prostitution (4:12). There isn't much hope in this book; if you dive into it thinking Israel will eventually see the light and turn themselves around, then you will be disappointed. The prevailing sense in Hosea is 'this unfaithfulness is never going to end'. And it didn't—Israel never did turn it around. Before long they were exiled and began receiving their comeuppance.

But the story of Hosea is not just the story of Old Testament Israel, it is our story too. We, like them, are also unable to conjure up what is required to make our hearts run straight and true. We can't make ourselves presentable to God. Nothing we can do will win him over or convince him that he should take us back. Our hope lies outside us. Like Gomer, the only hope for a wayward heart is a love which overrides our waywardness, a love which stretches out and covers our unfaithfulness. The story of the Bible isn't about humanity becoming loveable in order to be loved by God; it is about God's love for us making us more lovely.

The stories of *Beauty and the Beast* and Hosea remind us that we need a love from outside us to be restored, a love different from anything we have ever experienced. We are never going to be able to pull ourselves up by our own bootstraps. We have tried to straighten our wayward hearts and we couldn't do it—we read the books, we tried new strategies, and we got into accountability groups. But in the end, nothing much changed. The only way forward for us is for someone to love us who has seen us at our worst, someone who is not in denial about the ugliness and beastliness within, someone whose love will banish our ugliness and beastliness and make us human again. "God loves us in just this way—goes after us at our worst, keeps after us until he gets us, and makes lovers of men and women who know nothing of real love."[56]

Painful healing

Tolkien, author of *The Lord of the Rings*, was one of four friends who met weekly in C.S. Lewis's rooms, between 1922 and 1945.[57] They called themselves the Inklings, and they gathered together as friends to read, listen to and give feedback on each other's developing literary works.[58] The group, comprised of Tolkien, Lewis, Charles Williams and Owen Barfield, met together throughout the writing of many works, not least of which was *The Lord of the Rings*. Around the time Tolkien finished this epic work, C.S. Lewis began writing his own fantasy series, *The Chronicles of Narnia*.[59] Like Tolkien, he too drew an explicit connection between what people love and what they become, in the adventures of a young boy called Eustace.

In *The Voyage of the Dawn Treader*, Eustace, a mean and selfish boy, took shelter in a dragon's cave. He didn't know it at first, but before long he realised he was lying on a pile of treasure. He began to think about what he could do with it and how much he could take with him. Eventually, he fell asleep. When he awoke, he discovered something strange. "He had turned into a dragon while he was asleep. Sleeping on a dragon's hoard with greedy, dragonish thoughts in his heart, he had become a dragon himself."[60] He, like Sméagol, had been changed by what he loved. But while he liked the treasure, he didn't like how it had turned him into a dragon. It is here that the similarities between Tolkien's Gollum and Lewis's Eustace come to an end. There never was any redemption or restoration for Sméagol, only total and utter loss. But there is for Eustace, and it comes from the hand, or should I say the paw, of a lion called Aslan (who represents Jesus in Lewis's books).

When Aslan and Eustace meet face to face, Aslan tells Eustace he needs to get undressed. Eustace quickly realises Aslan is telling him he needs to peel his dragon skin off, so he gets to work scratching himself until the scales and skin peel off him like a banana. But, much to his disappointment, they only reveal another dragon skin underneath. He tries again and again but each time it doesn't work. Each time it simply reveals another dragon skin. Eventually, Aslan says to Eustace, "You will have to let me undress you."[61] Here is how Eustace recounted his experience:

> I was afraid of his claws, I can tell you, but I was pretty nearly desperate now ... The very first tear he made was so deep that I thought it had gone right into my heart. And when he began pulling the skin off, it hurt worse than anything I've ever felt ... he peeled the beastly stuff right off—just as I thought I'd done it myself the other three times, only they hadn't hurt—and there it was lying on the grass: only ever so much thicker, and darker, and more knobbly looking than the others had been. And there was I as smooth and soft and smaller than I had been. Then he caught hold of me—I didn't like that much for I was very tender underneath now that I'd no skin on—and threw me into the water. It smarted like anything but only for a moment. After that it became perfectly delicious and as soon as I started swimming and splashing I found that all the pain had gone from my arm. And then I saw why. I'd turned into a boy again.[62]

We don't have a cosmetic problem; we have a problem deep in our hearts. Like Eustace, our dragonish thoughts have turned us into dragons too. We can try hard to fix ourselves, but it is beyond our pay grade, beyond our ability. We just can't do it. Jesus, though, is an expert in the business of restoration and redemption. He specialises and delights in taking those who have been defaced and dehumanised by false loves and illicit lovers and turning them into glorious humans again, people who reflect and image the great and glorious one. You just have to let him love you and do his gracious work in you.

> *We all, with unveiled face, beholding the glory of the Lord, are being transformed into the same image from one degree of glory to another. (2 Cor 3:18)*

Scripture reading
Psalm 115, Hosea 1–4, Isaiah 44:1–20, Romans 1:18–32

For reflection and discussion

1. When do your idols seem to work for you? How can you tell they are becoming problematic?

2. This chapter referred to five areas which commonly get disordered in our lives. Which one do you feel the most acutely?
   a. Disordered loves
   b. Disordered dominion
   c. Disordered reality
   d. Disordered relationality
   e. Disordered relationships

3. What loves get disordered in your life? Who pays the price for your disordered loves?

4. When worship gets perverted, dominion gets inverted. Where does your God-given dominion get inverted in your life? Where can you see a healthy exercise of your God-given dominion feeding into your identity?

5. Think about your most common, go-to idol. What are all the lies it tells you? Why do you believe them?

6. What idolatry is most powerful in switching off your relationality? What does it look like when it happens?

7. How have your relationships been affected by the idols you worship? When have you treated other people as objects, rather than imagers of God?

8. Why is admitting your ugliness critical to you receiving the restorative grace and love of God? When have you struggled to own your beastliness (Ps 73:22)?

5. The true human

In their *Little Treehouse* children's book,[63] Andy Griffiths and Terry Denton tell the story of Professor Stupido, the greatest un-inventor in the world. As a child, Professor Stupido learned he had the power to un-invent things that annoyed him. His first un-invention was a robot which refused to play with him. He un-invented it by smashing it with a hammer. Then he discovered he could un-invent books by throwing them in the fire. Finally, he discovered he could un-invent anything he wanted to by pointing at it and saying a rhyme. He un-invented hot ice cream, flying beetroot, and the frogpotamus (it is a children's book after all). He ended up spending his days wandering around thinking of things he could un-invent and as he "un-invented more and more things, more and more people became unhappy with him."[64] But Professor Stupido didn't care what other people thought, he only cared about what he wanted. Eventually, while he was busy un-inventing things, the people of earth had a meeting and decided to un-invent Professor Stupido. They tied him to a rocket and blasted him to the dark side of the moon. The story ends with Professor Stupido shouting towards Earth, "You'll all be really sorry! I'll be back very soon once I've figured out how to un-invent the moon."[65]

As I read this children's book for the first time, I was struck by the parallel between the un-inventing Professor and humanity in the Garden of Eden. The unwinding of God's good, which first began in the fall of humanity, and the selfish motivation behind it seemed eerily similar to the work of Professor Stupido. However, while the book implies the people of Earth are free from the tendency to un-invent, we know from Scripture this is not the case. We are all guilty of un-inventing God's good. If anyone is to be tied to the rocket and sent away, it is us—and the rocket would need to be big enough for all of humanity. The other thing that struck me was the lack of redemption or restoration in the story. Professor Stupido was a bad person and the only way to deal with him was to get him away from everyone else. He needed to be banished.

Some of us have felt the bite of banishment. You know what it is like to be an outcast and not make the cut in a social group, at work, or perhaps even in your own family. Your brother or sister was the favourite and there was nothing you could do to win your parents over. Or perhaps you blew it and forgiveness was never freely given. You have felt separated and banished ever since. For some it is relational, for others it is both relational and physical. Whatever the situation, you know what it means to be living in a story with no redemption, no restoration. You remember the day they tied you to a rocket and sent you away. You can still feel the cold steel on your back.

Redemption and restoration

While we can find ourselves stuck in a story devoid of redemption or restoration, we are drawn to stories where they play a vital role. We buy books about them, we watch movies which centre upon them, and we attend the theatre to have them played out before our eyes. Stories without redemption and restoration don't tend to be very popular. It seems we don't have the stomach for a bad ending. Some time ago I watched the director's cut of *The Butterfly Effect*, a science-fiction movie where the main character discovered the ability to go back in time and change some of the harmful things that had happened to him in his childhood. But every time he changed something it caused a worse consequence down the track. This cycle repeated over and over as he frantically worked to correct the evils which had happened to him, but it became obvious that every action he took only made matters worse later in his life. While the cinema version of the movie had a happy ending, the director's cut was much more gut-wrenching. The last scene in the movie showed the character as a foetus in his mother's womb, taking the only option left to him to rectify the evil that had happened—he killed himself. His life ended in a miscarriage. The movie affected me for days. While I have never recommended anyone watch it, it was one of the most powerful movies I have seen. The whole movie was about a redemption which remained just out of reach of the main character. While he desperately wanted it, he couldn't quite get his hands on it, and death became the only option.

The reason why stories of redemption and restoration appeal to us so much is because redemption and restoration are part of the fabric of the universe. God's story, the main story, is a redemption and restoration story. It began amazingly, took a tragic turn, but is on track to finish even better than it started (Rev 22). Some may not know about it, or may not be interested in it, but that doesn't make it any less important. Who God is and what he is doing are the most important things for humanity.

If you go right back to the very beginning, redemption and restoration make their first appearance at the fall of humanity. While he had a plan before then (Eph 1:4), it was in that disastrous moment God put out his first press release about his plan to rescue humanity. It was amazing timing. In that moment, the hope of redemption and restoration was wedged in between humanity and hopelessness. Someone born of a woman would crush the head of the serpent (Gen 3:15). The devil would not have the last word. Neither would sin, guilt or shame. God had a plan to redeem, remake, restore, and revive his broken, messed-up world. And it wasn't going to be done remotely. A hero was going to come and rescue humanity.

Stop for a moment and notice the tender hand of God in the middle of a mess. He is not satisfied to send humanity away without hope. Sure and certain hope sustains us. When you cut your finger, you have a sure and certain hope it will heal (with a few exceptions). Most of the time you don't think twice about it. This kind of hope keeps us afloat, it keeps us going. If something bad happens, there is a way out. We might joke about something being hopeless from time to time, but when something is truly hopeless, even living becomes too difficult. God knows humanity thrives when there is hope, and we struggle when it disappears. Hope, redemption and restoration go together.

Fallen heroes

From that point on in biblical history, it's a mixed bag. Most of humanity continued to want to be in the centre of the story, and many of them did outrageously evil things (Judg 19). But there was also a scattering of heroes who were raised up by God to lead his people. They loved God and lived to serve him, his plans and purposes. Lots of good things happened under these leaders. But they weren't perfect. From time to time, they too wanted to be the centre of the story. You might be surprised at some of the illustrious people in this group. Moses, the great leader, got angry and publicly dishonoured God (Num 20:12). King David, the man after God's own heart, saw a naked woman bathing, called her up to his palace, committed adultery and then had her husband killed (2 Sam 11). Throughout the Scriptures we learn of people who got close to being the kind of hero we needed but, in the end, they fell short and left us disappointed. It turns out they, like us, had a darker side.

In the 1990s, my Grandpop (my father's father) became a Christian. It was a big deal because he was a hard man, a veteran of the Second World War. He was a heavy drinker and smoker, and could be violent in the house. He was also known to engage in gambling from time to time. But later on in life, Jesus changed his heart and with that came a thirst for God's word. He went to a local bookstore in his small town and bought the only Bible he could find, a children's illustrated story Bible. The next time our family visited, my dad noticed what he was reading and offered to get him a proper Bible. He gladly received his new Bible and began reading. The next time we dropped in I overheard him saying to my father, "Roland, I have been reading this Bible and it is full of scoundrels. I expected there to be heroes in it." In one fell swoop, he had summarised the story of human history—no one can get it right.

While good things happened when God worked through people in the Old Testament, their record left humanity wanting something more, something better. There were heroes, to be sure, but they were fallen, broken heroes. They did some great things, but there was always collateral damage. They just couldn't hold it together for long enough. Their only hope, that a standout rescuer would come, rang in their ears. The bitterness of evil and their disillusionment in fallen leaders left them longing for someone better who was not marred by their own weakness and sinfulness (Heb 7:27), someone with heroic power and character. In the meantime, they were left with a strange brew of disappointment and longing.

Have you ever tasted this strange brew? Perhaps it was your dad who served it to you. He was the one who was meant to be the hero in your life, the one who would anchor things and make you secure. But he didn't. He did some good things, no doubt. But you wanted more than a meal on the table or clothes on your back. You just wanted him to love you and tell you about it. For some of you, your dad did say he loved you, but he never backed it up with action. Or perhaps it was perverted love. He could be nice in front of others and treat you well at times, but his darker side was terrifying. You never knew when it would come out, or what he would do. He was meant to be your hero, but he ended up being both a hero and villain in your life. Even when he was being a hero to you, you couldn't think of anything but the villainous side, wondering when it would re-emerge. If this is you, then you know all too well what it is like to long for a better hero.

The Messiah arrives

As biblical history moved on, God warned his people about their disobedience to the covenant he had made with them and the very real prospect of their being taken into exile. The reading of this part of Israel's history is like watching a car accident—everything is in slow motion and there is nothing you can do to stop it. In the end, God's people continued their disobedience and were exiled. God had warned them their disobedience could end up with him not talking to them any more: "They shall wander from sea to sea, and from north to east; they shall run to and fro, to seek the word of the LORD, but they shall not find it" (Amos 8:12). And that was exactly what happened. While he didn't leave them bereft of revelation (they had all of the other inspired writings of the Old Testament), they didn't get anything fresh for 400 years. That's a long time. God's silence was deafening.

Yet, in the midst of the silence, hope lived on. The promise of Genesis 3:15 lit the fire of expectation that someday someone would come who would deal with the problems caused by Satan in the fall of humanity. We know hope lived on because it swirls around Jesus in the gospels. While the word 'Messiah' is absent from the Old Testament, the meaning behind the name, 'anointed one', isn't (Ps 2:2, 132:17). The Israelites expected that "one day God would send into the world an exceptionally great Person, a mighty Deliverer, One who would represent him in a very special sense. This coming great One was thought of, not as 'an anointed one', but as 'the anointed one', 'the Messiah.'"[66] He wouldn't merely be another in a long line of prophets, priests and kings. He would be *the* prophet, priest and king. The prophets foretold how the anointed one's rule would lead the world back to an Eden-like flourishing[67] (Isa 11 & 32).

If you asked a Jew who their hero was, who was going to rescue them from the mess they were in, they would have told you—the Messiah, the anointed one, the Christ. His name was not just an identifier, it was a title.[68] It said something about what he was coming to do. He wasn't just going to be another one in a long line of people who were mostly good. He would come and make things right. He was the quintessential hero in the eyes of the Jewish nation. For them, the name Messiah, or the Christ (John 1:41), was synonymous with the word hero.

Jesus is the hero the world is looking for, the one our hearts long for. We were made for God and we were made to be close to God. There is no better summary of what is normal for humanity than Calvin's: "The proper condition of creatures is to keep close to God."[69] It is normal to be close to Jesus and it is abnormal to be distant from him. Do you notice things going haywire when you and he are distant? Like a power plug and a socket, we belong together and will only be fulfilled when we are plugged into him. He is light (1 John 1:5), in him is life (John 1:4), in his presence is fullness of joy (Ps 16:11), and there is nothing as desirable as him (Ps 73:25). Pay attention to your longings, and take notice when you are drawn to him; this is how you have been made. There is a connection between the way you have been made and the way you experience life. Or, as Augustine put it, God has made us for himself and "our hearts are restless till they find rest in thee."[70] Your deepest longings are really a longing for Jesus.

The people waited and waited for their hero, their Messiah, to come. Then, under the cover of darkness, in a small country town, the creator of the world snuck in. While others were celebrating men who had become gods (the Caesars), the God who had become man was born. No fireworks, no fanfare, and no news coverage. So unusual, so unconventional, so … majestically beautiful. Jesus was born. He was the one they had been waiting for, the one their hearts were longing for. And he is the one you long for too, whether you realise it or not. The hero of God's story had arrived.

Different but better

I became a Christian over thirty years ago. In the time I have followed Jesus, I have learnt a bunch of things. One thing I've discovered in following Jesus is that you should expect the unexpected. Expect him to do things you don't expect, and expect him to do things you expect, but in an unexpected way. I am rarely on the money when it comes to the what and the how of God's work. I have also seen how God's ways and means are best. I have often found myself thinking, "Now I wouldn't have done it like that, but that was probably the best way to do it". Have you ever had the same thought? Ever found yourself thinking, "Now that was totally different to what I expected, but it was way better"? You never would have guessed it and you never would have planned it, but the outcome surpassed what you had imagined. This was what it was like when Jesus came to dwell among us.

Jesus was different from the Messiah that most people expected. For most of Jesus' life and ministry, he bumped into people who expected or wanted him to be something different from what he was. There were times the crowd wanted to "take him by force to make him king" (John 6:15), and another time when one of his closest disciples took him aside and began to rebuke him for suggesting he was a suffering Messiah (Mark 8:32). [Side note: if you ever find yourself feeling like you need to rebuke Jesus, sit down for a moment, take a deep breath and have a cold drink. Something has gone terribly wrong.]

We shouldn't be surprised at the misalignment between who Jesus was and what people expected him to be. The world had drifted a long way from what it once was. From his conception, Jesus was unconventional. He was conceived by the Holy Spirit in a virgin (Luke 1:35) and born in a manger because there was no room in the inn (Luke 2:7). The creator of the world, who made the world to be our home, was born in a feeding trough. Who would have thought? But this was all part of the master plan. We needed someone who would come and do things differently. It was a taste of things to come, a precursor to his work that reversed the curse of sin.

Reversing the curse

In the first four chapters of this book, I outlined the nature of the human condition and how we got here. In chapter one, I unpacked how sin entered God's good world and began unwinding it. Sin's best work, or should I say its worst work, was death, the ultimate dehumanisation of people made in the image of God. In chapter two, we looked at how shame snuck in with sin and insulated us from the help we needed—it shut us off relationally. In chapter three, we took a closer look at what happened in the fall and how, as relational worshippers, we committed adultery when we turned away from God to other lovers. Finally, in chapter four, we considered the effect our idolatry had on who we are, our identity. In the remainder of this chapter, we will look at how Jesus is the rescuer we need. He is our hero, our Messiah. He has come to reverse the curse by dealing with death, shame, our relationships, and our identity.

Death

In Jesus was life (John 1:4), vibrant, pulsating, overflowing, sustaining life. He created life in the beginning (John 1:3) and in him all things hold together (Col 1:17). All the rainforests, and colourful finches, and musicians and performers. Every living thing came from him and is held together by him. Remember the Garden of Eden? God's presence made creation flourish. Wherever Jesus' life-giving presence is, life abounds. Wherever he goes, people flourish and life happens. Even dead people can't stay dead when life itself touches them.

The Gospel of Luke tells the story of a woman on the way to bury her only son. She was a widow. She knew what death tasted like. She had already buried her husband; she had already experienced too many lonely nights without him. Now she was burying her only son and, with him, her material wellbeing and lineage. Luke's telling of the story is particularly vivid. Jesus was walking into town with a crowd just as the woman was walking out of town with a crowd, escorting her son's dead body to his resting place. From a distance, it would have looked like a faceoff. What would Jesus do? Good question. He had a lot of people with him. Perhaps he would pause for a moment, acknowledge the woman's situation and then move onto more important things. After all, for most of us, it makes sense to invest our time where we can get the most bang for our ministry buck. But not Jesus. In a moment, the crowds melted away and all he saw was the woman and her dreadful situation. "When the Lord saw her, he had compassion on her" (Luke 7:13). The crowds didn't matter. The only thing that mattered was the plight of the widow. He reached up, touched the burial bed the boy was lying on and told him to get up (Luke 7:14). Immediately he sat up and began to speak. The people who witnessed the miracle responded in awe and said, "God has visited his people" (Luke 7:16). God was not some distant force who had resurrected the widow's son remotely. He had come close. This is what happens when life itself comes close—dead people live again. Jesus versus death isn't a fair fight; Jesus' life dominates death every time.

Jesus' life reverses spiritual death too. One of the most well-known examples of this was Zacchaeus in Luke 19:1–10. He was a Jewish chief tax collector who worked for the Romans collecting taxes from his own people. He had become rich by ripping off his own nation. He would have been viewed in the same light as a murderer or robber.[71] As Jesus walked by one day, this wealthy extortionist decided he wanted to see this man he had heard about. But he was too short and there was a crowd in his way.

So he climbed a tree. And much to his surprise, Jesus came over. It turns out Jesus was keen to see him too![72] That day Zacchaeus had Jesus over for a meal and he was never the same again. By the time Jesus left, Zacchaeus was spiritually alive. In response to Zacchaeus' commitment to repay those he had defrauded four times, Jesus declared, "Today salvation has come to this house ... the Son of Man came to seek and to save the lost" (Luke 19:9–10). Jesus makes dead people live.

Wherever Jesus is, life happens. Cripples walk again, sinners are forgiven, people are raised from the dead, relationships get restored, and the demon-possessed get liberated. In short, the presence of Jesus causes people to flourish. Expect to see it. It can be no other way. It is irrepressible and unstoppable. A reminder of Eden.

Shame

In the incarnation of Jesus, God entered humanity's shame bubble. While God could have dealt with humanity at arm's length, he doesn't. He comes close in the person of Jesus—Immanuel, God with us (Matt 1:23). Jesus was born of a woman, just as God had foretold in the garden (Gen 3:15). "The Second Person in God, the Son, became human himself: was born into the world as an actual man ... of a particular height, with hair of a particular colour, speaking a particular language, weighing so many stone."[73] No one else was going to be able to reverse the curse of sin. No one else could save us. It couldn't be a fallen person or an angel[74] or even a robot—it had to be Jesus, "made like his brothers in every respect" (Heb 2:17). Our mediator and high priest needed to be a man (1 Tim 2:5). We needed someone who was truly human to come and save us. We needed another, better Adam. God didn't just come close to us in Jesus, he crawled into humanity's skin. Or as Calvin put it, "He is near us, indeed touches us, since He is our flesh."[75] Stop for a moment and consider how close he is to you; how, in his humanity, he is so intimately 'with us'. But that's only the start of his closeness.

As we read the stories about Jesus, we quickly see he is drawn to broken, messy people. This is a far cry from what we expect. We expect Jesus to have been in church all the time with the 'good people.' But he wasn't. He spent a lot of time with people who couldn't get their stuff together, so much so that he got a bad reputation for it. "Look at him! A glutton and a drunkard, a friend of tax collectors and sinners!" (Matt 11:19) This accusation is meant to hurt but, to those who count themselves sinners, it is the most sublime thought. No one needs a friend more than a sinner. Some of you know what it is like to publicly fail. You know what it is like to have those you considered friends drop you like a stone. Everyone liked you when you were the person they wanted you to be. But when you failed, they scurried off like mice when the lights are turned on. Or maybe your failure hasn't gone public. It's a secret only you and a few others know, and you live in fear of it getting out. I have good news for you: Jesus is a friend of sinners. You will never stand alone.

I think I can understand Jesus' enjoyment of broken, messy people. In the last couple of years, I have had the opportunity to help out in some drug rehab centres. It has been so refreshing. Everyone is there because they have made a mess of their lives and it is on the public record. In my work alongside the residents, there was a welcome absence of ducking and weaving and almost no hiding. They were broken and messy and wanted help. It was quite a contrast to what it can be like working with people in churches. The longer I work in churches, the more I realise there is no such thing as a messy church and a clean church. Every church is filled with messy people. The only difference between them is one church talks about their mess and the other doesn't. Jesus seems to have a penchant for the authentically fallen, those who are honest about being busted, messy and broken. And I get that.

Jesus wasn't just with us in that he walked around on the planet; he regularly touched those who were suffering. Jesus did not have a no-touch policy. One time, when he was in Bethsaida, "some people brought to him a blind man and begged him to touch him. And he took the blind man by the hand and led him out of the village" (Mark 8:22–23). While we don't know how long the man had been blind, we can see his friends wanted him to be healed. Jesus took him by the hand and led him out. Then he did something many of us would struggle with: He spat on the man's eyes, laid his hands on his eyes and healed him. Would you let Jesus get that close? Would you let him touch you like that? Jesus' touch is not evil. It is not the touch of someone stealing your innocence. It is a healing, restorative touch—a touch that makes things go right, not wrong. I think if he were here, he would physically touch you. And you wouldn't feel violated. No one ever felt violated by Jesus' touch, only loved and healed. When he touched people, it put them back together. It reversed the physical disintegration brought on by sin.

Jesus' touch also extended to the social outcasts, those who were unclean. He touched the untouchables. Mark tells the story of a "highly provocative and offensive encounter"[76] between Jesus and a leper. Lepers were untouchable because they carried a mysterious disease and were ceremonially unclean. They were to cry out "unclean" as they walked around, and were to live alone, separate from those who didn't have the disease (Lev 13:45–46). The leprosy that had disfigured this man's skin would likely have disfigured his person too. His embarrassment and shame were all too public and real for it not to influence him. How long had it been since someone touched him? We are not told. He knelt at Jesus' feet and begged to be healed. Jesus "stretched out his hand and touched him" (Mark 1:41). What? What did he do? If we were watching we would probably have thought, "Well, Jesus is done for now. He is unclean and he will probably end up getting leprosy. What a stupid thing to do." But much to our surprise, Jesus doesn't get affected by the man, the man gets affected by Jesus. He gets healed! The leper doesn't rub off on Jesus, Jesus rubs off on him. And he will for you too. He invites you to give him your worst. Hand over the contagion of your sin and shame—the worst of it. Let him get inside your shame bubble and touch your uncleanness. Let him get close. It won't wreck him. With Jesus, things work in reverse.

Relationship

I have four sons. One of the great joys of my life is watching them interact as brothers. Like any family, there are fights and disagreements but, at the end of the day, my boys back one another. I have never heard of any boy who has three brothers getting bullied for very long. Some time ago, one of my boys was being treated badly by another boy at school. In the end, it really got to him. In an attempt to help him one day, his younger brother pulled him aside to give him some pointers about how he could handle it. He told him, "What you have to do is get a scary look on your face like this. Then make your voice as angry as you can and tell them you don't like it!" His brother responded, "And what if that doesn't work?" He replied, "Then you go and get Thomas", one of their older brothers. He knew he always had backup. He knew the security of having someone older and bigger who can back you when you are in trouble.

You have a big brother too. I am not talking about a biological big brother. I am talking about Jesus. When we turned away from God and were unfaithful to him, we got ourselves into a mess we couldn't get out of. We were stuck, stained and unable to get clean. But Jesus, our big brother (Heb 2:11), didn't leave us stuck. He swung into action and got to work on our behalf. What he did was unexpected, yet sublime.

Jesus is the mediator, the advocate, the high priest we so desperately needed, one who is not hamstrung by his own failures. He was betrayed by one of his closest friends (John 13:18), arrested, tried for blasphemy, found guilty and sentenced to death. They flogged him, made him carry his own cross, and crucified him on a hill called Golgotha (John 19:17). In that moment, the groupies were gone, along with the cheers and adulation of thousands. Only five supporters were left, and the rest of those around him were either in the process of executing him or making fun of him (Mark 15:31). As he hung there, he bore all our sins in his body on the tree (1 Pet 2:24). The just punishment for our unfaithfulness to God was poured onto him. In that moment, Jesus was at his high priestly best. The God, Immanuel, who is so intimately with us became powerfully for us as well.[77] The author of life was killed (Acts 3:15). The only one whose acceptance matters was rejected. The light of the world was snuffed out by our darkness. The one who deserved only good carried all our evil. Jesus, the faithful one, sorted out our relational mess by dying for the adulterers. And his death brought about "lasting relational change between God and humanity."[78]

As Jesus died on the cross for us, something strange happened, something keen observers would have seen glimpses of in his ministry: the curse of death was broken. In that moment on the cross, as death knifed him, Jesus used his own death to turn death on itself and kill it (Heb 2:14). While the devil may have celebrated a great victory in having Jesus executed, he didn't know that when this "willing victim who had committed no treachery was killed in a traitor's stead ... death itself would start working backwards."[79] And it did. The first reversal was his own death—three days later, Jesus was raised from the dead (Mark 16:6)—then it spread to everyone who has ever, or will ever, put their trust in him.

By dying on the cross, our brother and saviour worked on our behalf to do what was necessary for us to be restored to our former glory. His death and resurrection are sure and steady anchors for our deep longings, for the reversal of the death in and around us—relational death, physical death, the slow death of a healthy body, death by addiction. All of them meet their match in Jesus. It's as if Jesus says to them, "Death and dehumanisation, you can stop right there. No more of your dastardly work." And then he gets busy undoing death's handiwork. Or, to put it positively, he gets to work restoring what has been broken and corrupted. Every bit of it. On the cross, he paid for your complete re-humanisation, body and soul. His resurrection guarantees it. All of the death you have tasted, and all of the death you will yet taste, is being unwound. Like surging waves undercutting a sand dune, eventually, it will all give way and disappear. But don't think you need to wait until heaven to get it. While we don't receive the fullness of what he purchased for us until then, it starts right now. Once you are connected to him, his life begins to flow to you and the effects of death begin to be reversed. You don't need to be afraid anymore (Heb 2:15). Death has been defanged (1 Cor 15:55). It is but a mere shadow.

Identity

Who am I? It is a question that has haunted humanity since the fall. In the beginning, we were royal representatives made to reflect the king wherever we went—we were children of the king. We were made to be connected to God and draw our identity from him. Before the fall, there was no lack of clarity. But the fall did away with all that. In a moment we went from ruling, royal children to estranged, enslaved children. Our identity took a massive hit and we have struggled with the question *who am I?* ever since.

Family—both our biological family and spiritual family—is one of the key places that helps us to know who we are. Jesus came to earth to gather God's estranged children and adopt them back into his family. In the opening page of his gospel, John highlights the importance of this part of Jesus' mission: "He came to his own, and his own people did not receive him. But to all who did receive him, who believed in his name, he gave the right to become children of God, who were born, not of blood nor of the will of the flesh nor of the will of man, but of God" (John 1:11–13). Sin left us estranged, isolated, orphans. We became whatever we worshipped. Jesus came to reunite lost children with their father. He did the work so you would be beloved children once again (John 20:17).

The Gospel of John tells the story of Jesus' interaction with a ruler of the Jews called Nicodemus (John 3:1–15). He came by night to visit Jesus because he was curious about him and wanted to know more. In the course of the conversation, it became obvious that Nicodemus, though highly educated, did not have the understanding he needed. He wasn't alive to God the way he needed to be.[80] He was probably an older man (John 3:4) who thought he knew all he needed to know, and thought he knew exactly who he was. But he didn't. He was one of God's estranged children. As the conversation unfolded, Jesus told him he needed to be born again. Nicodemus, a little befuddled by what Jesus had said, responded, "How can a man be born when he is old? Can he enter a second time into his mother's womb and be born?" (John 3:4) Don't be fooled by the nature of his question. I think Nicodemus could see what Jesus was up to; he would have known he wasn't talking about physical rebirth. What he seemed to be asking was how "an old man, decisively shaped by his heritage and firmly set in his ways, could possibly turn the clock back and start all over again as a new person."[81] It was a good question, but one Jesus had already answered. Behavioural modification won't bring the change you most deeply need. What you really need is positional change, you need to be adopted back into the family. Like physical birth, being born again is not just about being alive, it is about being alive in a family.

As John continues, we get two more glimpses of Nicodemus. The first is a teaser of things to come. In the midst of the Pharisees debating who Jesus was, Nicodemus piped up and defended Jesus, but was quickly slapped down (John 7:50–52). The next time Nicodemus appears, it is at such a significant moment that we can only conclude the new birth he and Jesus had talked about had happened. Jesus had been crucified and his lifeless body was hanging on the cross. Joseph of Arimathea had gained clearance from Pilate to take away the body of Jesus, prepare it for burial, and lay Jesus in the tomb. It was Nicodemus who helped Joseph with the task. "So they took the body of Jesus and bound it in linen cloths with the spices, as is the burial custom of the Jews" (John 19:40). To identify with Jesus in this way is quite a change from their first conversation. Somewhere along the line, he must have "decided to participate in the way of Jesus."[82]

Jesus changes people. But he doesn't do it by behaviour modification, he does it by making us alive and adopting us. Jesus gathers the lost (Luke 15:4), the estranged children of God, the spiritual orphans, and makes them part of his family again. While our estrangement from God leaves our identity at the whim of every gift, talent, idol we worship, or sub-culture we are part of, Jesus does something better. He brings us back into the family. You are now a beloved child of the most significant person in the universe. Your identity doesn't equal your performance anymore. As we deepen our connection to God, we become more alive to the person God made us to be.

A personal union

If Jesus offers grace, forgiveness, acceptance, love and life, then how do we get them? Be careful here. If Jesus' good gifts have turned into a commodity, it is a sign something has gone wrong. Jesus doesn't run some kind of cosmic supermarket where you can go and get what you want and he pays the bill. To approach Jesus and his gifts this way is to deal with him in the same way we deal with idols. We are in the centre and Jesus has good things which we need, which will help our lives to go the way we want them to. But Jesus won't let you treat him like an idol. His objective is not to be a supernatural courier who brings you good things, but to give you himself. Idolatry leaves us wanting things to make our lives go, but God doesn't give you things, he gives you a person—the person of Jesus. Everything you want, everything you need, is wrapped up in who he is. While you can be disconnected from him and still get a taste of his goodness (Matt 5:45), you can't have it in its fullness outside of deep, personal communion with him.

You can see this dynamic operating in the story of the rich young ruler. He came to Jesus with great possessions but lacking eternal life. It was the next thing on his list. So he asked, "Teacher, what good deed must I do to have eternal life?" (Matt 19:16) Jesus asked him if he had kept the commandments. The man replied by telling Jesus he had. Then Jesus said, "You lack one thing: go, sell all that you have and give to the poor, and you will have treasure in heaven; and come, follow me" (Mark 10:21). If the rich young ruler wanted eternal life, he would have to sell everything and give Jesus his allegiance. He wasn't up for it and he walked away disappointed. Can you see what Jesus is up to? He is highlighting how eternal life is found in him, not separate from him. It isn't a standalone commodity that you can acquire. It is something you get only by being connected to Jesus. Jesus himself is eternal life (1 John 5:20) and you only get it by knowing him (John 17:3).

This close

Someone may ask, "How close do you need to be to get the good things Jesus has?" Well, actually, you need to be joined to him. You need to participate in him, in his person. Like a dishwasher needs to be plugged into a power supply to be what it was created to be, you need to be plugged into Jesus to receive the goodness which will make you truly human. In other words, you need to be grafted in (Rom 11:17).

Imagine a broken-off branch lying in a garden, slowly dying. As it begins withering, it looks up to a tree next to it. It knows it needs the benefits which are flowing to the other branches on the tree or it will die. And it wonders, "How do I get those benefits?" There is only one way. It needs to be grafted in. Once it is grafted in, all the benefits which are flowing to the other branches on the tree will flow to it also. Why? Because when it is grafted in it becomes one with the tree. Over time, this union between the branch and the tree will become less and less noticeable until it is indistinguishable. Eventually, the branch and the tree will be seamless.

How do we get grafted in? In one sense, you can't do it yourself, it is something that needs to be done for you. Like the branch, someone needs to come along, pick you up and graft you in. But in another sense, there is something you can do. You can, by faith, be united to Jesus in his death (Rom 6:5) and be crucified with him (Gal 2:20). You may wonder, "How would I do that? Didn't he die over 2000 years ago?" Well, you can't do it physically, but you can by faith. You can count yourself crucified with him. To be united in Christ's death and be crucified with him happens when you die to yourself and your old way of doing life, and embrace a life of faith and trust in Jesus. In that moment, you become united to him, and his life begins to flow to you.

If you love him, you have been grafted in. He has given you a new heart with a new inclination. The corruption and fragmentation sin and evil brought to you is in reverse. He has begun putting you back together. Sin fragments, but Jesus heals and restores. Pay attention to his sweet work in your life. Making things whole is his speciality.

> *If you want to get warm you must stand near the fire: if you want to be wet you must get into the water. If you want joy, power, peace, eternal life, you must get close to, or even into, the thing that has them. They are not a sort of prize which God could, if He chose, just hand out to anyone. They are a great fountain of energy and beauty spurting up at the very centre of reality. If you are close to it, the spray will wet you: if you are not, you will remain dry. Once a man is united to God, how could he not live forever? Once a man is separated from God, what can he do but wither and die?*
>
> *C.S. Lewis*[83]

Scripture reading
John 1:1–18, 3:1–15; Luke 7:11–17; Mark 1:40–45, 8:22–26

For reflection and discussion

1. When have you felt the bite of banishment? When have you felt like an outcast?

2. We all hope for redemption and restoration. When has it felt beyond your grasp?

3. When it comes to fallen leaders, have you ever tasted the strange brew of disappointment and longing? How does your longing point to who Jesus is?

4. This chapter considered four areas where Jesus reversed the curse. Which one is the most meaningful to you personally? Why is it the most meaningful?
   a. Death
   b. Shame
   c. Relationship
   d. Identity

5. Where can you see Jesus reversing death in you? What is he bringing alive again?

6. Jesus was drawn to broken, messy people. Do you think he would have been drawn to you? Why/why not?

7. Your brother Jesus restored the relationship between you and God. How does it feel to have your relational problems with God sorted out on your behalf?

8. When have you treated Jesus' blessings like commodities? Why are they richer and more nourishing in the context of relationship with Jesus?

6. Becoming truly human

We live in a world awash with information. It comes at us all day, every day. The great fear of decades ago, that information would be controlled by totalitarian states, has given way to a world where we can't keep up. Everyone's an expert now. All it takes is a quick internet search or a quick instructional video, and anyone can be an expert on anything. We know stuff and, anything we don't know, we can quickly find out. But it is a specific type of knowledge. It is knowledge about things. We know how to fix things, what the Prime Minister is doing over the weekend, what is happening in London in real time, what is happening in our next-door neighbour's house, and the current state of the surf break at the Gold Coast. Knowledge about things gives us a sense of power.

But in the midst of this wealth of knowledge, we discover that we are particularly lacking in one area—the art of knowing people personally. It is a little surprising. After all, one would think that with all the social media and connectivity tools at our disposal we would be better at it. But we aren't. It turns out knowing about people is different to knowing them. We are experts at one, and not so much at the other. One is about the mastery of information; the other is about relationship. Unfortunately, the social media which held so much promise for knowing people deeply has only led to more knowledge about rather than personal knowing. Online connectivity promised to bring us closer but it seems to have done the opposite. We are "lonely in a social world".[84]

Sometimes we can settle for knowing information about God, rather than knowing him personally. When we settle, we fall far short of what God desires for us. He is interested in much more than our knowing *about* him; he wants us to know *him*. What's the difference? Distance, for one thing. You can know about someone from a distance, but you can't know someone unless you are close. You need to be in their inner circle. The closer you are to them, the greater the opportunity you have to know them.

When Jesus died on the cross, he brought us into the inner circle. Although they are all good and necessary things, the ultimate point of his death wasn't to remove our punishment, or clean our consciences, or free us from evil and slavery—he died to connect us to the person of God. This is the way the apostle Peter put it: "Christ also suffered once for sins, the righteous for the unrighteous, that he might bring us to God" (1 Pet 3:18). On the cross, Jesus opened up the opportunity for us to be united with God. Face to face. Person to person.

Union with Jesus

Our union with Christ is the mind-blowing culmination of God's history-long commitment to be with his people: from his presence in Eden (Gen 3:8); to his commitment to be with Moses (Exod 3:12); to his commitment to be with his people, Israel (Exod 29:45); to his reassurance of his personal presence at the call of Jeremiah (Jer 1:8); to the coming of Immanuel, God with us (Matt 1:23). God's intention to dwell with his people is clear. From start to finish, the covenants (aka relationships) God forms with his people follow a familiar pattern: "I will make my dwelling among them and walk among them, and I will be their God, and they shall be my people" (2 Cor 6:16). God is a God who is *with*.

Union with Christ is one of the New Testament's mega themes. You could dive into it by looking at the writings of Paul. He often uses the phrase 'in Christ' to describe the believer's relationship to God: "If anyone is in Christ, he is a new creation" (2 Cor 5:17).

Sometimes he will pile it up with multiple uses of the phrase in the same section of Scripture. In the longest Greek sentence in the New Testament, he uses it no less than eight times: "Blessed be the God and Father of our Lord Jesus Christ, who has blessed us in Christ … he chose us in him … he has blessed us in the Beloved … In him we have redemption … in Christ … to unite all things in him … In him we have obtained an inheritance … In him …" (Eph 1:3–14). Other times he uses the metaphor of being grafted in (Rom 11:17). As I mentioned in chapter five, grafting is the process of taking a twig, stick or bud and attaching it to another plant (called the rootstock) to make the two grow together. Once the stick is grafted in it can "share in the nourishing root" (Rom 11:17). Who is the nourishing root? Jesus. When we repent and believe the good news of the gospel, God grafts us in, and his life begins flowing to us.

Another place you will encounter union with Christ is in the writings of the disciple John. According to John, being united to the life of Jesus is what life is all about. In the middle of perhaps the most concentrated section of Scripture on union with Christ, Jesus compares our union with him to a vine and its branches. "I am the vine; you are the branches. Whoever abides in me and I in him, he it is that bears much fruit" (John 15:5). This mutual indwelling of God in us, and us in him, is a common theme in John's writings[85] and is teased out in many different ways throughout John 14–16.

Union with Christ isn't solely about salvation, our restoration depends upon it also. Stop for a moment and remember where everything started. Life, the abundant life of the garden, was found in the presence of God. Death was the result of disconnecting from life itself. If you want to be vibrantly alive as a person, you will need to be connected to Jesus. If you are to be the one God had in his mind's eye when he made you, then you will need the ongoing nourishment of his presence. This is the way we have been made. We simply can't be who we were made to be without him.

Union with Jesus is about relationship

The nature of our union with Christ is profound and mysterious (John 14:20). It's hard to get your head around, partly due to the concept itself. Another reason is connected to the nature of metaphors. Metaphors aim to make something visible that is invisible. They tend to say one thing really well, without saying everything. So whilst being grafted in, being branches connected to the vine, or being 'in Christ' help us understand union with Christ, they only tell us what union with Christ is, not how to do it. Why? Because most of the metaphors aren't personal and we, by contrast, are intensely personal beings, united to the tripersonal God.

There is one metaphor for union with Christ which stands above all the others because it is intensely personal—marriage. God's relationship with his people throughout Scripture, understood as a marriage relationship, breaks out in all its fullness in the work of Jesus. In the book of Ephesians, Paul makes the direct connection between union with Jesus, and the union between a husband and wife. "'A man shall leave his father and mother and hold fast to his wife, and the two shall become one flesh.' This mystery is profound, and I am saying that it refers to Christ and the church" (Eph 5:31–32).

The one flesh union of marriage (Gen 2:24) helps us understand how we are to operate in union with Jesus. While a physical union is part of being one flesh, it is much more than that. In our culture, we can conceive of a solely physical engagement between two people, but that is not how God created it to be. Sex is not merely physical; it is deeply personal. In healthy marital sex, the fullness and intimacy of physical knowledge are matched by intimate, personal knowledge of one another. Two people have sex, not just two bodies. Sex is always personal and always involves the whole person. It was created by God to be the ultimate expression of the intermingling of souls, an intermingling which God intended to happen on every level. It is one of the reasons why the Old Testament tends to refer to loving marital sex as "knowing" one another

(Gen 4:1), and substitutes the words "lie with" (Gen 39:7) or "go in to" (Gen 16:2) when the sex is not about reciprocal intimacy.[86] This is why it is right for a spouse to hesitate when their partner wants sex in the midst of unhealthy relational dynamics. It simply isn't meant to be that way.

Marriage is about knowing and being known. In marriage, one whole person gradually comes together and intermingles with another whole person. This terminology, knowing and being known, is used in Scripture to describe our relationship with God. "To be known by God is to be known intimately and personally."[87] Over and over Scripture highlights the importance of knowing God personally (Jer 9:23–24) and being known by him (Amos 3:2, Matt 7:23). Sometimes knowing and being known by God appear together: "You have come to know God, or rather to be known by God" (Gal 4:9); "Now we see in a mirror dimly, but then face to face. Now I know in part; then I shall know fully, even as I have been fully known" (1 Cor 13:12).

In union with Christ, our whole person intermingles with the person of Jesus. I was reminded of this reality during an extended prayer and worship time at a place called Ravensbourne. There is a magnificent 180-degree view and a short rainforest walk nearby. As I was walking through the rainforest, I approached a bird standing on a branch of a fallen tree. As I got close it flew a couple of metres further up the track and I lost sight of it. I was stumped. How could I lose sight of it over that short distance? I looked and looked until I finally found it. It was hard to find because it was a similar colour to the rainforest. The penny dropped. That bird was in the rainforest in a completely different way to how I was in the rainforest, in my blue jeans and coloured t-shirt. The boundary between the rainforest and the bird was much less clear than the line that divided the rainforest and me. This is a little of how marriage and union with Christ are meant to be. Neither individual disappears as a person, but the boundaries between us blur as we open ourselves up to each other.

The engine room of relationship

Self-revelation

Knowing and being known is the mechanism within relationships that makes them go. It happens when people are personal and reveal themselves to one another. You can visualise this using the following illustrations:

The cup on either side represents each person. Inside their cup is everything which makes them who they are. Almost everything that makes them who they are is non-physical, it is invisible (this is why the cup is not clear). These things include how they respond emotionally, how they make decisions, what they love, what they are passionate about, their gifts and skills, their preferences, how they talk to others, their personality, and their strengths and weaknesses. While most of what makes us uniquely us is not visible to the naked eye, people will always be able to know some things about us (for example, through our body language) whether we like it or not, because we are personal by nature. The clear bottle in the middle is the space in which people reveal themselves to one another and engage in the process of knowing and being known.

Becoming truly human 119

Knowing and being known begins when one person takes a risk and 'goes public' with something about themselves, by pouring it into the self-revelation bottle. Whilst this part of them is now known by the other person, relationship isn't happening yet. Relationship depends on what the other person does next.

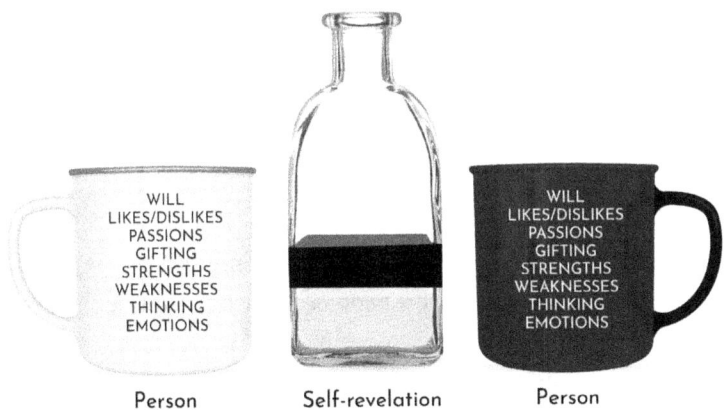

If the other person chooses to do the same, then you have the possibility of relationship because two people have been personal with one another. But it still isn't happening yet. People can know and be known by each other deeply, and still not be in relationship.

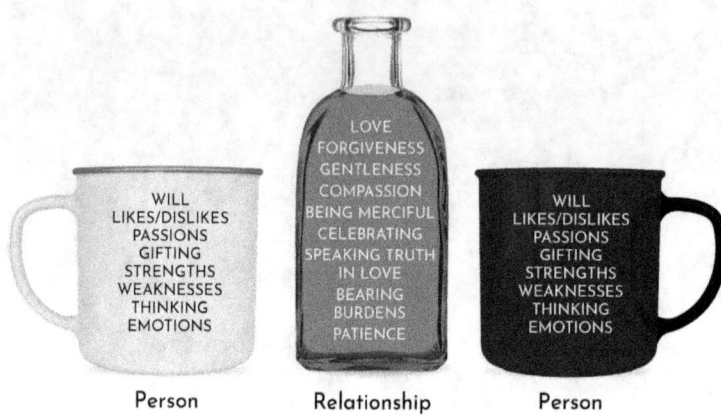

| Person | Relationship | Person |

In order to convert this self-revelation into relationship, the self-revelation of both people needs to intermingle. The way this happens is when each person moves towards each other through classic relational activities, such as loving one another, showing compassion, being merciful to one another, speaking truth in love, and so on. When this happens, you have two people operating personally and relationally with each other. Their personhood has intermingled a little. They know and are known by each other a little bit more. As they repeat this process over and over, the depth of their relationship increases.

God is a self-revealer

God is a self-revealer who reveals himself in order to "establish a personal relationship with his people."[88] It isn't merely a character trait; it is an expression of his personhood. And he doesn't wait for us to go first—he always leads, taking the first step, and has done so since the very beginning. Whilst he is God, the way he reveals himself is similar to the way we do—through words (see Exod 34:5–7 for a powerful example) and actions (Exod 6:6–7). And, while God reveals himself throughout Scripture, there is no purer expression of who he is than the person of Jesus, "the radiance of the glory of God and the exact imprint of his nature" (Heb 1:3).

Jesus is the most concentrated self-revelation of God, sent to restore relationship with his estranged children.

When we enter into relationship with Jesus, we discover his self-revelation goes beyond the initial forming of relationship and becomes the way in which it operates. Self-revelation is an essential part of friendship: "I have called you friends, for all that I have heard from my Father I have made known to you" (John 15:15). As we engage in relationship with God, we discover the upright really are in his confidence (Prov 3:32)—they get the inside word. This is the promise of Jesus: "He who loves me will be loved by my Father, and I will love him and manifest myself to him" (John 14:20–21). If you love Jesus, the Father loves you, and Jesus shows more of himself to you. Stop and think about that for a moment.

Like other relationships, you don't get to know everything about Jesus all at once. There is always more to know, and as you walk with him, he will let you in on it. This very thing is what Paul longs for, "that I may know him and the power of his resurrection, and may share his sufferings, becoming like him in his death" (Phil 3:10). When it comes to communion and union with Christ, there is always more for you—more depth, more life, more revelation, more enjoyment.

We need to get accustomed to being deeply personal with Jesus. In a marriage relationship there is the formation of a relationship and the doing of the relationship. The wedding ceremony is the official formation of relationship, the marriage is the doing of relationship. The announcement of "husband and wife" at the end of a marriage ceremony doesn't mark the completion of two becoming one, it marks the beginning. Now that they have been united as one by a ceremony, they need to become one in practice. Husbands and wives need to "live into"[89] the reality they began by forming the covenant of marriage with one another. In some ways, being united with Jesus in his death is like a wedding ceremony. It is the formation of a deeply personal relationship between us and God.

But, like a wedding, it is only the beginning. The purpose of our union to him is ongoing communion with him.[90]

Blockers to being personal

At the end of Genesis 2, there is a statement about Adam and Eve which is both sublime and tragic: "The man and his wife were both naked and were not ashamed" (Gen 2:25). It is sublime because the thought of being fully known and not ashamed is idyllic. But it is also tragic because it shows us what we lost; it is so far gone we struggle to even imagine what it would be like. We have no reference point. This kind of world existed for a time, but was quickly followed by sin and shame, and we have been ducking and weaving ever since. It's not that we hide all the time. Deep down, we want to be seen and known for who we are. But we are erratic. One moment we are happy to be seen and known, and the next we're not. Sometimes we hide for years.

We have good reasons to hide—or at least we think we do. Our actions are not completely random. There is a logic that drives us. It is a dangerous world after all, and the dangers we see make us skittish. Before we look at some simple ways we can be personal with Jesus, we will briefly look at five common blockers.

Shame

Shame is probably the biggest blocker to being personal. Shame is the sense that we are less than human because of something we have done, something done to us, or something associated with us.[91] We feel like we are not good enough, dirty, or worthless. In a shame-filled state, being known is simply not an option. The risk of being rejected is far too great. So we hide from ourselves, and others. Those stuck in a shame pattern often don't talk about what is really going on inside them. People ask them how they are going and they say, "Good thanks", when in reality they are not going well at all. We can operate similarly in our relationship with God. We turn up at church, sing happy worship songs, join in the prayers, listen to the sermon, and give financially. But we never talk to God or anyone else about what is really going on. We are a mess.

In difficult pastoral situations, after people have shared some deep struggle in their life, I often ask, "Have you talked to God about that?" Most of the time they answer no. I then follow up with another question: "Why not?" Most of them reply, "I'm not sure". I believe them. When it comes to sins and sufferings and God, we often don't connect the dots. Sometimes it is because our relationship with God is a little distant or dysfunctional. We don't think to tell him the things we would tell a close friend because it is 'different'; he doesn't feel like a close friend. Other times it is shame. We don't like talking about shameful things. Talking about shameful things makes them feel more real. It brings them closer. But, whilst this is uncomfortable, it is an essential part of God's process of dealing with our shame. It needs to become real so he can invade it. Leave it in the ether and no one will be able to get to it. Hiding never helps. Get your dirty laundry out, put it on the table, and talk about it with him.

Idolatry
The effect of idolatry on our knowing and being known by God is quite straightforward. In idolatry, we turn away from relationship with God to relationship with something else. In doing so, we make it clear to God we neither want to know him nor be known by him. We have another lover to whom we are giving ourselves, and not much of us is left. We have turned our ear to listen to the words and deceptive promises of an idol, not God. In the end, we become dead and impersonal, just like the idols we revere. Relationships with idols always make you less personal and less relational. Sin is the empirical evidence you have given yourself to someone or something else, and the process of knowing and being known by God has come to a standstill.

Past hurt

This is a thorny one. Most of you would know what it is like to hesitate being personal because of hurt in the past. A sinful world is a dangerous place to be open, to be personal, to self-reveal. You remember the time they hurt you. You were open and you shared your life with them. For a short time, they respected and loved you. But then *that* day came. A bull in a china shop doesn't come close to describing what happened. They took the piece of you which you had given to them and smashed it on the ground. Then they trampled it. They beat that part of you until it was only a smear on the pavement. It hurt so much you made a vow: *No one will ever do that to me again*. Self-protection became the name of the game. *Nothing bad will ever get in here again*. But it is lonely in there. Your defences didn't just keep evil out, they kept love out too, and you desperately long to be loved. You want to be personal but it is just too dangerous. What to do?

For some of you, it feels like it was God who hurt you. There is a hidden rift between you and God that you don't talk about to anyone.[92] Your life hasn't gone the way you wanted it to go and, in your mind, it is largely his fault. Perhaps it was the way he created you and the ongoing struggles you face, or the family you were born into. Or maybe you served God faithfully over the long term and everything changed in an instant. An undiagnosed condition was discovered, a tragic accident happened, or someone did something brutal to you and you have never been the same since. You can identify with the disciples in the storm on the sea of Galilee (Mark 4:35–41). In the aftermath of what happened to you, it didn't seem like Jesus cared if you drowned either. As far as you are concerned, he didn't do anything to help. You actually don't think he is very good, but you dare not say it in church or in your prayers because, well, you just don't say that. It isn't appropriate. So you don't really talk to him anymore, at least not about what matters most deeply. You don't open yourself up and trust him because he might hurt you again.

Laziness or avoidance

Sometimes being personal with God is blocked by laziness or avoidance. Relationships take work—there is talking, listening, and waiting to be done. If you want to be personal with Jesus, you will need to work out what is happening inside of you, talk it out with him, push through your own shame, and then wait for him to respond. Often it is easier to do nothing. Sit on the couch and watch television, get another glass of wine, get another hit. Don't talk about it, don't look at it, and don't deal with it. Just find a way to avoid it.

A little while ago, Laura came to me for some help. She was grieving the death of her close friend. Whilst all deaths are painful, this one seemed worse. Laura's friend was young and she left behind a young family. Laura struggled deeply with losing her friend but, rather than face up to her grief and wrestle with it, she opted for distraction. Anyone who has had to deal with grief would understand. I certainly did. It wasn't a particularly toxic type of distraction, just television. When space opened up in her life to work through her grief with Jesus, she would watch comedies on television instead. She knew she had to face up to it one day, but she pushed that day back whenever she could. She knew talking about her pain, hurt and anger would only make it more real, so she didn't. Then finally, unbeknownst to me, on one particular Saturday, she resisted the temptations of distraction and escapism and fronted up to Jesus with her grief and pain. She took her grief out, put it on the table between her and Jesus, and they talked about it. When we caught up next, she told me all about it. She told me how exhausting it was, and how good it was. She called it work, and it sounded like it. It wasn't fun, and it wasn't easy, but it was good. Her grief wasn't over, but it was on the table, and she and Jesus were talking about it.

Unfamiliarity

There are times when being personal is difficult because we have been brought up in family or societal cultures which have actively discouraged it. In these cultures, people often place a high value on being calm, keeping a tight rein on emotions, and maintaining a 'stiff upper lip'. One key way to spot these cultures is by the way people within them say nice things about others behind their backs but never to their faces. I have seen this dynamic in operation at countless funerals. When the opportunity comes for someone to say a few words they take it with both hands and say everything they wanted to say to the deceased while they were alive but didn't. It is a precious moment, deeply personal, and a little sad. The presence of this dynamic at funerals in particular highlights the collision between our desire to be personal, the fact we don't always know how to go about it, and our fear of navigating the other side of it. So we don't do it. We opt for safety. Being personal feels weak. It feels vulnerable. While there are times when we are willing to take the risk, in general, our culture steps in and says, "Don't express your feelings. Don't show your weakness. Don't talk about what is really going on for you. Pretend you don't care. She'll be right mate. Don't worry about it. It will get better. Have another drink." So we all fall into line and stay silent and learn to live with the nagging thought that we have walked with the people around us for years but we don't really know them.

Henry grew up in a loving family in Australia. His parents were of British extraction, and his father was a busy, hardworking farmer. From the outside, he was a member of a fine family that regularly showed hospitality to outsiders. They were an accepting, affectionate lot. All of the children were loved by their parents, and they knew it. But Mum and Dad never told them. It just wasn't a thing. In Henry's house, people never got personal. Ever. Sometimes he noticed his parents struggling in their relationship, but they never talked about it. You just didn't do that. The unwritten family rule was, "You don't talk about anything personal." In its place was sarcasm (something which has the run of the house in many families). At its best, sarcasm provides the opportunity to express affection without being personal. In Australian culture, if we rip on you, it means we love you. In Henry's family, being personal was foreign, being sarcastic was familiar, and his family's culture left him in the dark regarding how to be personal.

Being personal with Jesus

In this final section, I want to look briefly at three simple ways we can operate in union with Jesus: remaining in his love, listening to him, and talking to him. I encourage you to read slowly and resist the urge to think, "Yep. I know that." Take the time to consider how each of these can be done in personal and impersonal ways.

Remaining in his love

Remaining in Jesus' love is like the marriage which follows the wedding. Just as a husband and wife need to remain in each other's love, we need to remain in Jesus' love. This is a significant part of Jesus' teaching in John 15. In the early part of the chapter (15:1–7), he uses the phrase 'abide in me' before swapping over to abiding/remaining in his love (15:9–10). Abiding in Jesus is synonymous with abiding in his love. Jesus doesn't want you to feel loved once; he wants you to know you are loved unceasingly. He wants you to remain in his love. But how do we do it? Jesus tells us how: "If you keep my commandments, you will abide in my love" (15:10).

Before you flip the switch and begin thinking about this in a non-relational way, let me remind you of a couple of things. The first is this: Jesus is telling you how to remain in his love; he wants you to stay in an intensely personal and relational space. Secondly, be careful not to put the cart before the horse. Good works don't lead to Jesus' love after salvation, any more than they did in bringing about your salvation (Gal 3:3). God was gracious to you and formed relationship with you while you were still a sinner (Rom 5:8). Obedience flows from relationship, not the other way around. Don't forget this order. When relationship is downstream of obedience, obedience becomes impersonal and non-relational (Matt 15:8).

Keeping Jesus' commandments is about honouring Jesus and valuing what is important to him. He is not an impersonal force. We relate to him as one person to another, always taking his concerns into account.[93] If you want to do relationship with a person, then you will need to care about what they like and dislike. Jesus tells you what he likes and dislikes. What we do next is not just a random act, it is personal.

Imagine I came home from work one day and, whilst having coffee with my wife, I suddenly yelled out at the top of my lungs, "Yee-ha! Woo hoo! This coffee is the bomb!" Can you imagine how she would respond? She would probably look puzzled and ask me what the heck I was doing. Imagine I did it every time we had a coffee together. It would get pretty annoying, wouldn't it? Eventually, she would say something like, "I don't really like it when you do that. Can you stop?" Can you see what she has just done? She has gone public with what she likes and dislikes – she has self-revealed, and I need to work out what I will do with it. Her going public with what she thinks about my actions changes things the next time I feel tempted to yell out about a coffee. Yelling out about coffee is now more personal; if I do it again, it will say something about what I think of her.[94]

Keeping Jesus' commandments is also about staying faithful to him. Every relationship functions by a set of rules. Break the rules and you break the relationship. This is the reason why the bride and groom make vows to one another in a wedding ceremony. They are the ground rules for their relationship. One mainstay in wedding vows is the commitment to exclusivity. It is a fundamental component of any healthy, functioning relationship. You simply can't have a healthy marriage with someone who is continually unfaithful. It is the same in our relationship with God. Disobedience and sin are the fruit of relational unfaithfulness. They are the consequence of an affair with a false god. Obedience is the fruit of rightly-ordered love. Remember what Jesus said? "If you keep my commandments, you will abide in my love" (John 15:10). Following Jesus' commands is about being faithful to him. Disobedience is a deliberate moving away from his love, from relationship. This verse is like someone who tells their spouse, "Stay faithful to me and you will remain in my love." Of course they will! That's how you do it. No wonder you stay in his love when you obey him—there is no other possibility.

Listening to Jesus

The first recorded words from a human don't appear in Scripture until Eve is given to Adam (Gen 2:23). Up until then, God has been doing all the talking. He spoke creation into existence (Gen 1), he declared how he was going to make humanity (Gen 1:26), he gave Adam and Eve some general instructions (Gen 1:28–30), gave Adam instructions concerning the garden (Gen 2:16–17), and then declared it wasn't good for the man to be alone (Gen 2:18). A lot of talking happens before we read human words, and a lot of important things are said. This is a reminder of who God is and that what he is doing and saying are the most important things for humanity to pay attention to. Before we speak, we need to listen; any speaking that doesn't follow listening will be out of place. We need to be people whose speaking is shaped by listening; as Isaiah prophesied, "The Lord GOD has given me the tongue of those who are taught" (Isa 50:4).

If you want to operate well in relationship, then you will need to be a good listener. We tend to talk too soon. This is why Scripture encourages us to be slow to speak (Jas 1:19). I wonder if you have ever had this experience: you're in a group of people when someone new joins in. Normally, when new people join a group, they listen for a while before speaking, in order to understand the flow of the conversation. But not this person. At the first pause in the conversation, this person jumps in and says what they want to say, without any respect for the group or current topic of conversation. They should have listened first, but they didn't, and they walked roughshod over other people in the group. Listening helps locate yourself in the situation you find yourself in. Good listening leads to good speaking. This is true in our relationship with God too. Jesus highlights this when he says, "If you abide in me, and my words abide in you, ask whatever you wish, and it will be done for you" (John 15:7). When we listen well to Jesus, we will know how to speak to him, and what we ask will be done for us.

Truly listening is not as easy as we think. We often believe we have it all sewn up. We study Scripture, we take courses in theology, we read the Bible regularly, we listen to sermons, but somehow, in the midst of it all, listening can evade us. We can think we are listening when we aren't. Scripture's repeated appeals to listen highlight how tricky it can be (Isa 55:2, Ps 85:8, Matt 11:15, Rev 2–3). We tend to listen to what God says as merely information rather than the words of the almighty one, our father and friend.

True listening requires us to be personally engaged and attentive to the one who is speaking. We listen well to God when we adopt a nimble posture, ready to interact and respond to what he says. Whenever we hear God and don't do what he says, there is a problem with how we are listening and the fruit is self-deception (Jas 1:22). This disconnect is often the result of approaching Scripture theoretically, as concepts and truths to be learned, rather than the very words of God. Scripture is not merely theory, it isn't simply theology, and it isn't mainly an instruction book for how life works best. Scripture is a personal message from God to you, applied by the Holy Spirit. At times we are inattentive because our hearts have set our attention on something other than God (Ezek 33:31). We are more focused on our agenda and what we want than we are on God. This is the spiritual equivalent of thinking about the next thing you want to say before the other person has finished talking.

The best way to hear the voice of Jesus is by reading the Bible. We hear Jesus most clearly and assuredly as the Spirit brings the Scriptures alive to us. Those who love Jesus don't just hear words or theology when it is read, they hear the person behind the words. He arrests their attention and stirs their hearts. The best way to have a conversation with God is to pray with your Bible open. Read Scripture and talk to him about what you are reading. You will be surprised at how easily it will turn into a conversation.

Talking to Jesus

Jesus could read people like a children's book. He knew everything about them and could see into their hearts (John 2:24), but he was never smug or arrogant about it. When people came to him asking him to heal their child or relative or friend he never said, "Yep. I already knew about that. Tell me something I don't know!" He knew it all, but he was never a know-it-all. Rather, he talked and listened to those who came to him. He had normal conversations with them, and he wants to have normal conversations with you too. God wants you to talk to him about everything (1 Thess 5:17, Phil 4:6).

Have you ever been in a situation where you have heard some exciting news about a close friend before they could tell you themselves? If so, then you probably know how it goes. The next time you get together, they ask you if you heard the news. You sheepishly answer, "Yes." The excitement written all over their face drains away and a disappointed look takes its place. So you quickly jump in, "No, no. Tell me. I want to hear *you* tell me." So they launch into their telling of the news with all the gusto and excitement they might have had before. In this moment, it isn't about information. You already had that. It's about your friend. You want to hear them tell the story because your excitement at the good news is not about the news itself, it is about what the news means for your friend. As they retell the story to you, the information comes alive in the one you love. This is how God listens to you. Talk to him about you. Tell him everything on your heart (Ps 62:8).

Talking to God is not mainly about data transfer, it is about relationship. If it were about data, it would be redundant because

God already knows everything. When you talk to God, you are doing relationship with him. You can see this dynamic in Jesus' teaching in the sermon on the mount; he warns those listening about the danger of repetitious words and reassures his listeners "the Father knows what you need before you ask him" (Matt 6:8). Unfortunately, these particular words of Jesus have stifled countless prayers; "Why would I need to pray if he already knows everything?" The reason it is a prayer-killer is not because of what Jesus is saying, but the way we understand prayer as mainly data transfer. This is the farthest thing from Jesus' mind. Look at the next thing he says: "Pray like this" (Matt 6:9). According to Jesus, God's knowledge isn't a barrier to prayer, but a reason for it. Your Father knows everything you need. You should talk to him.

It turns out that sharing what is on our hearts is trickier than it seems. You would expect that having someone on call, who loves us and gives their attention to us whenever we want to talk, would lead to a deluge of speaking and demand a great deal of listening. But this is not always the case. While many people talk to God, the personal nature of our speaking to him is as sporadic as it is in our human relationships. Sometimes we are superficial, sometimes we dive in a little deeper. Shame, idolatry, pain and escapism have their effect on the way we talk to everyone, including the way we talk to God.

We begin really talking to God by admitting we don't quite know how to do it. When we come to faith, prayer is a language we don't know; talking to someone we cannot see, hear, or touch is a new experience for us. As we move into this new world of communing with God, we understand more clearly what the disciples were getting at when they said to Jesus, "Lord, teach us to pray" (Luke 11:1). And Jesus does; not only in the Lord's Prayer but throughout all the Scriptures. When it comes to being personal in the way we talk to God, there is no better place to learn how to do it than in the Psalms. There we learn how God talks to us and how we can talk to him.⁹⁵ Let's take four well-known types of talking to God and look briefly at how the Psalms help us do it in a personal way.

1. **Confession**

   "Against you, you only, have I sinned and done what is evil in your sight, so that you may be justified in your words and blameless in your judgment." (Ps 51:4)

   All sin is first and foremost against God. Recognise your sin is not mainly a judicial problem, but a relational problem between you and God. Use personal pronouns—I, you, me—and own your sin as a personal offence to God. Be as specific as possible and don't hold back on describing the darkness of what you did. His love and forgiveness are waiting for you.

2. **Lament**

   "You have put me in the depths of the pit, in the regions dark and deep. Your wrath lies heavy upon me, and you overwhelm me with all your waves." (Ps 88:6–7)

   Pour out your pain to God. Tell him how it is for you. About a third of the Psalms are laments (Psalm 88 is arguably the darkest). There is much help in the Psalms for those who are suffering. Vivid images and words, which capture the contours of human experience, abound. Mine them and harness them to help you speak your pain to God. Tell him about the darkest, least presentable bits of you (Ps 137:9). If you think your pain is his fault, tell him about it. He can handle it.

3. **Praise**

   "My soul longs, yes, faints for the courts of the Lord; my heart and flesh sing for joy to the living God." (Ps 84:2)

   The Psalms don't just speak of the greatness of God, but of the psalmist's enjoyment of God's greatness. You can make prayers of praise more personal by including your enjoyment of God in them. If you want to be more personal when you praise God then don't just tell him what he is like, tell him what he is like and why you like him.

4. **Petition**

"Incline your ear, O LORD, and answer me, for I am poor and needy. Preserve my life, for I am godly; save your servant, who trusts in you—you are my God. Be gracious to me, O Lord, for to you do I cry all the day." (Ps 86:1–3)

Make your petitions personal. Don't just ask for what you need or want, tell God why you need it or want it. Why is it important to you? Why is God your only hope? What trouble do you need God's intervention in? What pain is your trouble causing you?

The Spirit brings Jesus close

Have you ever wished you could have been with Jesus in person? Ever wanted to touch him, see him, or simply be with him physically? If you answered yes to any of these, then you are in pretty good company. The thought of not having Jesus around physically wasn't a pleasant one for the disciples either (John 16:6). When he talked about leaving them, it filled them with grief. But they need not have worried. Jesus was Immanuel, God with us. He wouldn't leave them as orphans (John 14:18). Whatever he had organised they could expect it to be something which would bring God close. That is who he is. That is his nature.

Jesus told the disciples, "It is to your advantage that I go away, for if I do not go away, the Helper will not come to you" (John 16:7). What Jesus was saying was it was better for the disciples to not have him and have the Holy Spirit, rather than have him and not have the Holy Spirit. Do you believe this? I suspect some of you want to, but the thought of his physical presence is too enticing. But stop for a moment and consider the limitations of a physical Jesus. For starters, only about eight people would be able to be around him at any one point in time. Then you would have the problem of needing to share him with everyone else on the planet. And what if your ten minutes with Jesus came around and you had a shocker like the disciples often did? What if you completely misunderstood him, or did something embarrassing, what then? It would be hard to come back from that. A physical Jesus is good, but the Holy Spirit living inside of you is better.

One of the key things the Holy Spirit has been tasked to do is unite us to Jesus and help us to know him deeply. He is the one who brings the real-time, lived experience of union with Christ to us—"In that day [when the Spirit is given] you will know that I am in my Father, and you in me, and I in you" (John 14:20). He bears witness in our spirit that we are God's children and he causes us to cry out, "Abba! Father!" (Rom 8:15–16)

So get after it. There is more for you in knowing and being known. More closeness. More communion. More richness. More satisfaction.

Expect to know him better.
Expect to enjoy him more.
Expect to become more you than you have ever been.

I will not leave you as orphans; I will come to you...
In that day [when the Holy Spirit comes] you will know that
I am in my Father, and you in me, and I in you.
(John 14:18,20)

Scripture reading
John 14–16

For reflection and discussion

1. What is the difference between knowing God and knowing *about* God? Where can you see each of these types of knowledge in your life?

2. Knowing and being known are the engine room of relationship with God. How is this similar or different to the way you engage with God?

3. What do you love most about being close to Jesus?

4. Which blockers to being personal get in between you and God? Describe what this looks like in your life.
    a. Shame
    b. Idolatry
    c. Past hurt
    d. Laziness or avoidance
    e. Unfamiliarity

5. Do you feel like it is God who has hurt you? What do you do with that feeling?

6. When have you abided in God's love? What was it like?

7. How much do you care about Jesus' likes and dislikes?

8. When you listen to God, do you listen to him as one person to another? How could you be more personally engaged in the way you listen to God?

9. Of the four categories of speaking to God, which ones need to become more personal in your life?
   a. Confession
   b. Lament
   c. Praise
   d. Petition

7. Interrupting rehumanisation

I have always enjoyed building things. From sheds to furniture to house renovations, doing something physical and creative with my hands has always been a passion of mine. As my sons grew up, one by one, they would become interested in what I was doing and want to help out. It was a familiar pattern. They would venture out of the house, watch what I was doing, and then eventually ask if they could have a turn. At first, I resisted because I knew their involvement at such a young age would only result in more work on my end. But soon enough, I came to realise the higher value of working together, than of getting a job done efficiently.

As I handed over a particular part of a project to them, I would say, "Here you go. You can do this bit. Here is how you—" At which point they would interrupt me and say, "It's okay Dad. I know how to do it." I would quickly reply, "Yes, I know you think you know how to do it. I just want to make sure you do. This is how to do it." Then they would say, "DAD! I KNOW HOW TO DO IT!" At this point, provided they weren't going to hurt themselves, I would step back and let them go ahead. I knew they didn't know how to do it and I knew they would probably make a bigger mess, but they were determined to do it themselves, so I let them. Most of the time I was right.

We can be a little like this when it comes to our own restoration. While we have seen and tasted the effects of God's restorative work, we still tend to want to take the steering wheel back from him and do it ourselves. But, like my sons, our attempts to fix the hole in our soul only tend to make matters worse.

What happened to the self

In the beginning, humanity's connection to God was intact. We were oriented to God, we imaged him, and who we were was settled. But sin came in and disordered everything it touched—and it touched everything. Something happened deep down in humanity. Something happened to the self. Before sin, the self was quiet, out of sight and out of mind. No one noticed it. But when sin arrived, the self got noisy and stepped into the spotlight. This is how it works; when the self is healthy it doesn't draw attention, but when it gets unhealthy it takes centre stage.

In some ways, the self is a little like your stomach. You probably don't think about it or notice it when it is full and healthy. But if it gets empty or becomes sick you will be hard-pressed not to think about it. As imagers of God, we are designed to draw our value and identity directly from God himself. Before the fall, our connection to God was unbroken and our self was quiet and content. But as soon as we disconnected from God, our self began to scream. It got noisy because it was no longer receiving a steady diet of the good things which come directly from God.

The self becomes noisy under the weight of pride and shame. The noisiness of the self under shame is easily observable in the actions of Adam and Eve, post-sin. They hide behind fig leaves and bushes, and then behind excuses and scapegoating (Gen 3:7–12). It's pretty obvious something is going on. Pride, whilst just as noisy internally, is a little harder to pick on the outside because proud people don't like to show any weaknesses or shortcomings. Thankfully, the Scriptures clue us into the noisiness of pride. We find one of the most succinct descriptions of it in the short Psalm 131:

> O Lord, my heart is not lifted up;
>   my eyes are not raised too high;
> I do not occupy myself with things
>   too great and too marvellous for me.
> But I have calmed and quieted my soul,
>   like a weaned child with its mother;
>   like a weaned child is my soul within me.
> O Israel, hope in the Lord
>   from this time forth and forevermore.

While the psalm speaks of the humble one who is at rest, the nature of the proud person is clear. They reach out for things too great and marvellous for them and are like an unweaned, fussing infant waiting for a feed from their mother. While the proud person may look like they are in control, the reality is there is a great deal to do, and it makes for a busy, anxious self (1 Pet 5:6–7). Humility, on the other hand, is restful, calm, and quiet.

Some time ago, I remember a mentor of mine talking about someone he ran into at a party. He observed how this person was "comfortable in his own skin". He was comfortable in who he was and he was able to be himself without pride puffing him up or shame sidelining him. What a sublime thought. Stop for a moment and think about it. Can you imagine what it would be like? For many of us, pride and shame are such close companions we can't envisage what it would be like to live without them. Imagine never feeling bad about yourself, never hesitating to say something because you thought you didn't have much to say. Imagine a world without those self-confident, arrogant people who shut you down, or those thoughts you have—not just of failing, but being a failure. Imagine a world without pecking orders. Imagine a world where you don't feel as though you have to control things to be okay.

It will happen in all its fullness one day. You can be sure of that. But in the meantime, in the in-between, you can trust Jesus to lead you in the direction of being comfortable in your own skin, of operating freely and normally out of who you are.

Unfinished business

In the past two chapters, we turned a corner. We turned our attention away from the effects of sin, shame and guilt and towards the coming of the true human—Jesus. We saw how the one who kicked us out of the garden did not stay there without us. He followed us out and ended up with us, in human flesh, kicking the dust for thirty-three years. And, as he did, he went to work reversing the effects of the fall. Death became life, sickness became healing, guilt became innocence. Everywhere he went, things seemed to go into reverse. Light came into the darkness and people began to see in ways they had never seen before. Life began breaking out.

But it gets even better. By his death on the cross, Jesus went beyond forgiveness and opened up the opportunity for humanity to be united to him. What a stunning thought. How humanity can be united to Jesus and included in the life of the Trinity is profound indeed (John 14:20). While we may not understand all the ins and outs of how it works, one thing we know is true—the blessings and benefits of Christ flow to us through this union.

The union we have with Jesus isn't an impersonal connection or vending machine. It is a personal, intimate, relational connection through which Jesus nourishes us. As we participate in Christ and enjoy communion with him, his life and the benefits he has purchased flow to us. This is the mechanism by which we are restored. Our journey to becoming fully human, to being the person God had in his mind's eye when he made us (Ps 139), is dependent upon this union with Jesus.

One would think a union like this, between the infinite God and tiny humans, would be the end of us. To the untrained eye, it looks for all money like we will be overlooked, overshadowed, or a forgotten member of this partnership. But, in our union with Jesus, we don't get obscured by him. Rather, our identity is enlarged by him because it now involves another person.[96] You will never be more *you* than when Jesus is in the centre of your life.

Whilst Jesus has made the way for some amazing things, it isn't long before we run into a bit of a problem. We quickly realise there is much more to this process of becoming truly human than we thought. What God has done for us and what he is doing in us is the most important thing about who we are,[97] but it is not the only thing that has to change if we are to be restored. We will need to be constantly engaged. And we shouldn't be surprised—if our restoration is dependent upon our union with Christ, and our union with Christ is all about relationship, then we will need to be actively involved. There is no other way. It's simply not possible to have a relationship with anyone, let alone God himself, where one of the parties is not actively engaged.

The work of Christ on the cross profoundly changed who we are. We went from estranged family members to children. From guilty to clean (1 John 1:7). From rebels to friends (John 15:15). We have been given a new heart with new desires (Ezek 36:26–27), and the Spirit by whom we cry, "Abba! Father!" (Rom 8:15). But we are unfinished. It isn't that the work of Jesus is incomplete. It is complete! It's just that God means for us to live into who we are. Or, as John Piper puts it, he means for us to become who we are.[98] We have an unshakable new identity in Jesus which cannot be taken away from us, but it is one which we are prone to forget (2 Pet 1:9). In the words of Paul Tripp, we get identity amnesia.[99]

Saving ourselves

God's call for us to live into who we are is the stage on which many of the battles for our restoration take place. It is an ongoing tussle between what Jesus has done for us and the effects of indwelling sin and shame. Whilst Jesus' work on our behalf is powerful, pride still tempts us to be someone great, while shame tells us we are no one. It is dizzying indeed.

Part of what makes this battle so tricky is the way guilt and shame distract us from our core problem. In the aftermath of sin, guilt screams at us and our shame condemns us. Both of them are parasites which draw their life from our bad behaviour. They are like massive neon signs saying, "This is what is wrong with you. Your behaviour is simply not good enough." Under the weight of guilt and shame, we can easily slip into thinking, "If my defective performance got me into this, then improved performance will get me out." And so we get to work. But it doesn't work. It never does, because the root of our problem was never performance, it was relational unfaithfulness—and you can't fix relational breakdown with improved performance.

Adam and Eve knew what an aching, noisy self was like. In the aftermath of their sin, they never said sorry, and they never asked for forgiveness. When their sin, pride, and shame all turned up at the same time in the same place, they saw, in no uncertain terms, how important it was to be acceptable in the eyes of others. They quickly got to work in an effort to save themselves (Gen 3:7–13). And we are just the same. When guilt and shame show up, we follow their example and work to find ways to be righteous without paying attention to how our efforts will eventually trap us. It is a toxic vortex.

Once you have swallowed the lie that performance is both the problem and the solution, then you have stepped onto the approval treadmill. And in the early days, it feels like it works. You have some control again. It is a nice, predictable combination of law and maths; when you do something wrong all you need to do is something right and it will counter the evidence against you. But before long, you realise your improved performance just doesn't go deep enough. Shame speaks to you in the core of your being and says you are not okay. It tells you the problem isn't mainly what you have done—you have a problem with who you are. You are not acceptable, presentable, or respectable. It leaves you in pain, out of control, and stuck.

We so desperately want to be okay in the depths of our being, and we want someone to tell us we are okay. The kind of approval

I am talking about here is not the surface level variety you see in a child looking for their parent's approval after performing a task, or a pastor looking for sermon feedback from the congregation. What I am talking about is something far deeper than success or failure. What we really want is for someone to look into the depths of who we are, see all the wonder and the horror, and love us. Our desire for someone to tell us we are okay isn't so much connected to not being good enough; it's relational in nature. We want to be loved. But we know what we are truly like, and we often conclude the risk of being known and not loved is too big. It is safer to be likeable and impressive and win approval, even though we secretly know it won't satisfy us.

Living for approval is about fixing your identity rather than living into your true identity. We all step onto this treadmill from time to time. No one is exempt. This human tendency to fix ourselves by making ourselves respectable began at the fall and continues to this very day. It is one sure way to interrupt God's restorative, redemptive work in your life. Your aching, noisy self will never be ultimately soothed by improved performance. Only a real-time, loving relationship with God can do that. While there will be times where God warns you about living by approval, and other times where he presses in and disciplines you, expect him to give you the wiggle room to live this way if you really want to. But you need to be careful.

Coram Deo

Our tendency to live for the approval of others is a distortion and corruption of the way we have been made. We were created to live our lives *Coram Deo*, a Latin phrase which means "before the face of God".[100] It captures the idea that God is everywhere, and he sees and evaluates all we do.[101] There is nothing we can do outside of his presence. But living *coram Deo* does not mean an impersonal relationship. Rather, it is intensely personal. The mention of God's face in the Scriptures always denotes his intensely personal presence.[102] For example, Moses' relationship with God is described in these terms: "The LORD used to speak to Moses, face to face, as a man speaks to his friend" (Exod 33:11). To live before the face of God is intended to be a "fully personal relationship."[103]

Whilst humanity always lives in the presence of God (Ps 139:7–12), we were made to live in the intimately personal presence of God. This much is clear from the opening pages of Scripture. After God created Adam, he put him in the garden (Gen 2:8), the place where God dwelt, the first temple. God did dwell throughout the rest of the earth, and he did dwell throughout the land of Eden, but there was something different about God's presence in the garden. It was closer and more personal. It was an intimately personal presence that humanity was designed to enjoy. We see clues of this in Genesis 2, and then in Genesis 3:8 where, in the midst of the unfolding fall of humanity, at the time of the day when the cool breezes were blowing, God was taking a walk. He wasn't just generally present; he was richly, personally present. In the garden, Adam and Eve could talk and walk with him. Adam and Eve were made to be in the presence of God—and you were too. It was being in the intimate presence of God that made Adam and Eve truly human.

You are hardwired to draw your value and your identity from God himself. Genesis 1 teaches us a fundamental fact about humanity—we were made in the image and likeness of God (Gen 1:26). We were made to reflect the object of our worship just as a mirror bears the image of whatever it reflects. If a mirror bears the image of something great, it will look splendid. If it bears the image of something hideous, it too will be hideous. Scripture makes this direct connection between the object of our worship and our identity. If we are oriented to God in love and worship, we will be "transformed into the same image from one degree of glory to another" (2 Cor 3:18). If we love and worship something worthless, we too will become worthless (Jer 2:5). "We become what we worship."[104]

The god in whose presence you reside will be the one you draw your identity from. Consider mirrors again, and the basic principles of using them. Firstly, mirrors image whatever is closest to them. If I took my bathroom mirror, put it inside my friend's shed and then complained about how I couldn't see my reflection in it at my house, everyone would think I was crazy. Mirrors are always in the immediate presence of whatever they reflect. Whatever is closest to the mirror will be the object which occupies the most space in it. Secondly, mirrors reflect whatever they are oriented towards. A mirror that points away from you will never reflect you. It has to be oriented to you. As imagers, we were made to be personally close and oriented towards God, reflecting him.

When humanity turned from God, we didn't stop imaging and we didn't stop drawing our value and identity from the one in whose presence we lived. While we kept operating in the same way we always had, two key things changed: the one in whose presence we lived, and the mechanism through which we drew our value and identity. As imagers, we always live in the presence of someone, and whoever's presence we live in shapes our identity. That someone becomes the puppet master in our lives, either knowingly or unknowingly, and we dance to their tune. We no longer lived consciously in the intimate presence of God, and the drawing of our identity transitioned away from our relational status and became connected to behavioural performance. This is the engine room of approval.

How approval works

Approval and presence

You seek approval from the person in whose presence you live. In order to gain a fuller understanding of the

relevance of presence, let's take a moment to consider the various ways we live in other people's presence.

We can physically be in the presence of others—this is the easiest one for most of us to understand. If you are standing next to someone, you are in their presence. When my wife and I arrive home from work and see one another, we are in each other's presence. Humanity has, at times, been in the physical presence of God. They have seen him and heard him. Theologians call these events theophanies. The most significant theophany was the coming of Jesus in human flesh. In that day, people were able to be in the physical presence of God. They could talk with him, touch him, and see him.

But being in someone's physical presence doesn't always guarantee we are *in* their presence. You can be with someone and not be with them at the same time. Let me explain. Have you ever been in a conversation with someone when they became distracted by something behind you? There you were, sharing your heart with them, and all of a sudden they were looking past you. Or worse, through you. They stopped looking at you and they stopped listening to you. You didn't even know whether you should go on. In a moment, you stopped being in their presence. They had gone, even though they were still physically present. Presence isn't just about proximity or physicality.

On the other hand, we can be in someone's presence even when we are not physically with them. Sometimes, when we think about others we can have a sense of their presence even though we may be physically distant. Memories are an example of this. Most of us have probably been to a funeral and the gathering that often follows. We have joined in with others as they recounted funny stories or the humorous quirks of our lost loved ones. And, in some ways, as we remember them they are present with us. It is beautiful and sad all at the same time.

Outside of physical presence, perhaps the most profound way to understand how we live in the presence of others is via the metaphor of voices. We all have an internal dialogue which runs through our heads during the day. It is made up of the things we say to ourselves, the things others have said to us, and what we imagine others are saying to us. Words are powerful. Death and life truly are in the power of the tongue (Prov 18:21). But there is another facet to it. By carrying the words of others around in our heads and ruminating on them, there is a sense in which we are living in their presence, for good or for ill. Jesus makes this explicit connection: "Abide in me, and I in you … If you abide in me, and my words abide in you" (John 15:4,7). To carry Jesus' words with you is in some way carrying Jesus with you. When we remember what he says, we remember him. When his words remain in us, he remains in us.

Like a hologram, a person's words can transmit their presence to us and can shape who we are, whether we are with that person or not. When I was 16, my Nana made an off-handed, critical comment about my physical appearance and I carried those words for years. Whenever I heard them in my mind, I saw her face and heard her say the words all over again. Many of us still remember the words said to us by our grandparents, our spouses, our fathers and mothers and so on. They rattle around inside our heads like rusty bolts in an iron tin. Some of them linger long after those who said them have passed away. When you boil it down, there are only three options regarding whose presence you will live in: your own, other people's, or God's. Sometimes we can switch between the three, or even try to keep two happy at once. But, at the end of the day, those three are your only options.

Approval, systems, and false reality
When you sign up to living for the approval of others, you get an entire system with it. Firstly, living for approval requires a moral code by which you will operate; there are things you do which earn you kudos, and other things which will earn you demerit points. Unfortunately, as we will discover in a moment, this moral code

is much more fluid than we would like. It can change from time to time, and from situation to situation. Most of the time you will have some kind of awareness of what the rules are; other times, they will shift and change without your knowledge and it will feel like you have walked into an ambush. Secondly, any system with a moral code will have its own unique expression of guilt and shame. When you comply with the moral code your deeds will be deemed righteous; break the code, you are guilty and deemed a bad person. Finally, in each approval system, there is a system of atonement by which those who are transgressors can work their way back to the right side of the law.

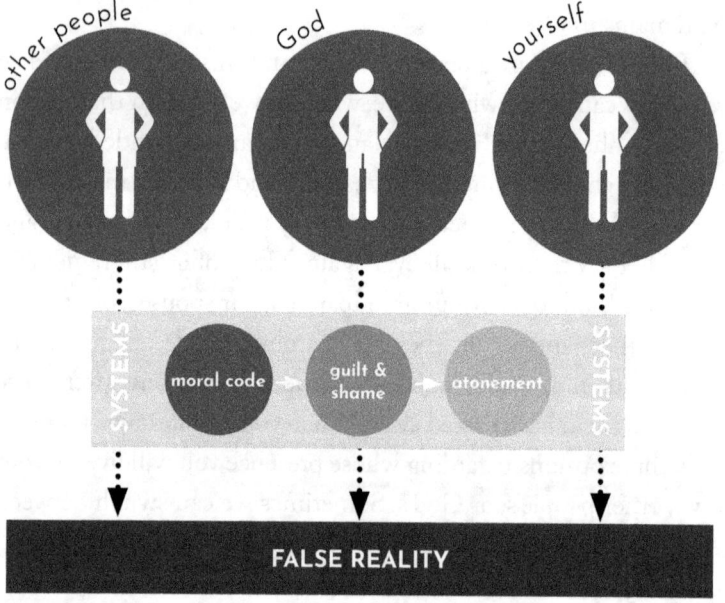

Whilst living for approval involves a whole system, the systems themselves don't correspond to reality. The moral code may bear some resemblance to God's law, but it is a perverted version; the guilt and shame are based on a defective moral law, and the system of atonement rescues you from one fate but not from your true predicament.

Approval destinations

Like the arrow in the diagram suggests, living for the approval of God, others, or yourself will take you somewhere. You will end up becoming a particular type of person. If you live for the approval of others, you will become a people pleaser who struggles with the fear of other people's opinions. If you live for your own approval, you will likely become a perfectionist. If you live for the approval of God, you will likely become a religious legalist.

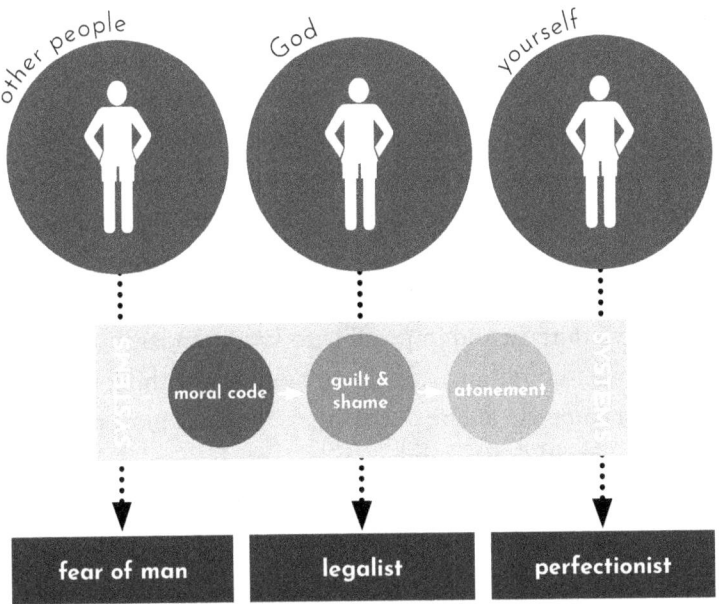

The shape of approval

Let's stop for a moment and consider the different ways seeking approval can show up in our day to day lives.

Living for our own approval

A person who seeks their own approval believes their standard is the only one which matters. They have a high moral code with its own internal logic. But the development of their moral code isn't a democratic process. They don't listen very much to what others think is right or wrong. Sometimes other people may comment on the moral law which the person adheres to, but the individual rarely ever pays attention to what other people think. The person decides what is right and wrong. Their law is the law above all other laws. Whilst they tend not to proclaim their moral code publicly or foist it on others, they will be fierce adherents themselves. They are hard workers and are often successful at fulfilling the overwhelming majority of their moral law. But for them, close enough is never good enough; it is 100% or it is nothing. Sometimes they harbour quiet pride or cold anger because they are doing things the right way and everyone else is getting it wrong.

When they fall short of their moral code, these people feel a great deal of guilt and shame. Their experience of failure can be confusing for people around them because their observers are not operating by the same moral code. The guilt and shame they feel don't make sense and it seems self-inflicted. Observers are often left befuddled, wondering why the person has imposed such stringent, seemingly arbitrary, and impossible to keep standards on themselves. To get everything right except one minor thing and then feel like a complete failure doesn't make sense to most people. It is a self-oriented death spiral.

What is their system of atonement? Sometimes they punish themselves. They might hit themselves, or do harmful things that lead to negative consequences because they feel as though they deserve it. Much of this self-punishment takes place in their internal world where they berate themselves for their failure. Sometimes it spills out of their mouth in an effort to persuade others of their badness. In the end, the only way out of their system is to pick themselves up, dust themselves off, and try harder in the hope that one day they will get everything right. Their little wins spur them towards this goal, even though it remains stubbornly out of reach. Living for your own approval is like chasing a mirage—every time you get closer, it moves further away. You never quite get there. It is a lifelong journey but you will never arrive at your desired destination.

Living for other people's approval

Of all the approval options, identifying the moral code in this system is the most difficult task of them all. While the standards which come from ourselves and God are quite static, the standards in this system move all over the place. They change depending on the person, the group, the composition of the group, the time of day, what has just happened prior to the conversation…the list is endless. It is endless because it has to account for all the constantly changing variables associated with relating to people. Added to this is the pressure to work out what other people want; this system is about winning their approval after all. We look at a frown or a glance away, and try to work out what the person is thinking and what is wrong. Sometimes these reactions are meaningless and we end up down the garden path because we have attributed a meaning that the cues were never intended to carry. The instability inherent in people's opinions and moods makes winning people's approval a constantly moving target. We sometimes find ourselves agreeing with philosopher Arthur Schopenhauer who wrote, "Other people's heads are too wretched a place for true happiness to have its seat."[105]

Unfortunately for those who live for the approval of others, their own guilt and shame are as murky as the moral law they try to follow. If it is hard to discern what people are thinking about you, then it will be hard to know when you have crossed the line. There are times when it is obvious—someone retorted, "that was a stupid thing to say", or they stopped talking with you after you did what you did. But these moments of clarity are dwarfed by all of the moments when it is unclear. We wonder, "Does that person have a problem with me? Have I done something to offend them? Do they think I am stupid?" Our shame mixes in with a lack of clarity and we end up feeling bad about things which were never a problem in the first place. We end up living in the fog of the oft-quoted saying:

> I am not who I think I am.
> I am not who you think I am.
> I am who I think you think I am.[106]

When it comes to the system of atonement, we are left with three options: a public flogging, trying harder, or some combination of the two. Some opt for a public flogging. They condemn and criticise themselves publicly. They say sorry multiple times. They think their public criticism of themselves will prove their righteousness to the world. They think their failure can be compensated for by meting out the appropriate penalty to themselves. They hope their earnest condemnation of themselves will sway the judges. Other times, they may just cut their losses and redouble their efforts to win the approval of others. They work harder to please, they try harder to be wise or the one who makes other people laugh. They do whatever they can to win back the approval of others—but they rarely ever know, with any kind of enduring certainty, if they have succeeded.

Living for God's approval

This may be a strange one for some of you. You may be wondering, "Aren't we supposed to live for God's approval?" Well, yes and no. There is a sense in which we are to seek to please our Father (1 Cor 4:5) but, in terms of winning his approval of who we are, sin has nullified that possibility. That doesn't stop some people from trying to win God's approval. Those people don't live their lives before a father, they live their lives before a judge—and this judge requires nothing less than perfection. These people are required to obey all of the law. No exceptions. The law they are to follow is clearly revealed in the Bible so they carefully search it and follow it in order to win God's favour. They pray fancy prayers, engage in self-sacrificial obedience and fast. Whatever they do, they believe they can win God's favour by being good. But they can't see the forest for the trees. What they have missed is an accurate understanding of the root of their problem. Their core problem is not compliance; their core problem is their relational unfaithfulness to God, which led to a failure to comply. Even if it were possible, compliance would not resolve their problem because the essence of their problem is not moral, it is relational. They are not rightly relating to him.

The clarity of God's moral law makes the guilt and shame of those living for God's approval rather stark indeed. God is the Holy Lord of all, and nothing we can offer him as sinners is acceptable in its own right. Everything is tarnished. Everything is infected in some way by sin. When it comes to living for God's approval, our experience is similar to robbers getting caught red-handed holding the bags of loot. Nothing we do will ever be good enough, and God knows everything and will see our every failure. The pressure is immense and exhausting. We simply can't get rid of our guilt or avoid becoming more guilty. We secretly hope that some of our good deeds might somehow outweigh the bad things we have done, but we know it doesn't work like that.

It is hard to see where atonement comes from in a legalist's religious system. Those who operate within these systems know God demands nothing less than spotless perfection, and they know they haven't been perfect. Their only hope for redemption rests on a rewards/punishment system. Try really hard, do well, and you will be blessed. Disobey or blowout and God will be after you. Fear is a close companion and weariness is inevitable, for there is no end of evil and sin needing to be driven out. There is not even time to sleep. It is an endless game of whack-a-mole; the moment you get on top of one thing, something else pops up. You are left hoping that God would cut you some slack because of how hard you have been trying. But he doesn't. He is a hard taskmaster. In the end, only the more disciplined people seem to enjoy some success. The rest give up in despair, knowing they will never be disciplined enough.

A caution
I have one caution. As you reflect on the shape approval can take in your life, be careful not to assume you are in the clear too quickly.

Some of you may have thought as you read, "No. That's not me. I don't think I have a problem with approval." But slow down for a moment. While it is possible you don't have a problem with approval, it may be that these characterisations don't resonate with you because you are winning at the approval game—for now anyway. You may be ultra-disciplined, talented, hardworking, and able to hit almost any mark you or others set (at least in your opinion). You may have had times where other people commented on your composure, skill, charismatic personality and confidence, wishing they were able to do what you do. But if this is you, be careful. Whilst you might think you are free of that struggle, you could still be on the same approval treadmill.

The alternative

When it comes down to it, there is one thing each of these systems has in common. Whether it is yourself, others, or God—someone is watching you. You always live in the presence of an observer. You have a judge who is watching your every move, a judge whom you have to please or you will be in trouble. You know what it is to sense their judgemental gaze and hear their voice bouncing around in your head. You live your day in their presence, responding to their demands (or what you think their demands are). You aren't you. You are a puppet on a string. You are what they want you to be. Pause for a moment and reflect on these questions:

> Who gets the most airtime in your life at the moment?
>
> Whose gaze do you sense? What look do they have on their face?
>
> Whose voice is the loudest in your head? What does it sound like? Is it loving and reassuring, or angry and harsh?

Living for approval is a trap. You are like a hamster in a wheel. You run faster and faster, and get more and more tired, and you go nowhere. Many of you are desperate to get off because you simply can't keep going anymore. Or for others, it's like being stuck in a casino and still thinking you can win against the house. Sure, no one else has won but you believe you are going to be the exception. If this is you, I urge you to look through the cheap thrills of approval and see the futility underneath. Choose to hop off that wheel. Don't back yourself to win an unwinnable game. You just don't have what it takes. Small victories belie final defeat. You won't win. In the end, no one wins.

Living our lives for approval couples our performance to our value. It links our behaviour to our identity. God's plan of restoration involves uncoupling these in you. And not because behaviour doesn't matter; it does. It's just that God has a bigger plan for you than a mathematical link between what you do and who you are. We can see how he did this uncoupling for the apostle Paul. Under the pressure of comparison with others Paul wrote, "But with me it is a very small thing that I should be judged by you or by any human court. In fact, I do not even judge myself" (1 Cor 4:3). Commenting on this section Tim Keller writes how Paul "sees all kinds of sins in himself—and all kinds of accomplishments too—but he refuses to connect them with himself or his identity."[107] Does that sound attractive to you?

What you and I need is not a behaviour change, but a positional change. We don't need to go down to the local bookstore and purchase more self-help books in order to be better. And it isn't about trying harder either. Neither of these approaches will fix the hole in your self; the hole is too big. We need an action from outside of ourselves. We need a positional change, not a behavioural change. What do I mean by that? The nature of the gaze you live under needs to change. You need a different tone in the voice which is speaking to you. In short, you need a shift from operating under the eyes of a judge to operating under the eyes of a father. Identity doesn't come from what you do, it comes from who you are related to.

When Adam and Eve sinned, they became estranged from God. They were his children, but when they turned from him relationally, all that was left was a holy, righteous judge. That was what he became to them. What they really needed was to get back in the family and ask the father to help them with the predicament they found themselves in. But they didn't. And one can understand why. If you're holding the contraband there is no more precarious place to be standing than next to the cosmic law enforcer. So they did their level best to be respectable, to get themselves back on the right side of the law. It didn't work. Adam and Eve simply didn't have the ability to do what needed to be done to get back into the family. But they didn't know how rich in mercy God actually was (Eph 2:4). God would be the one to do something. In the fullness of time, he would come in the person of Jesus, live the life we should have lived and die the death we should have died. He hung naked on the cross to purify us and cover our shame. And we now have the opportunity to be adopted back into his family.

In uniting us to himself, Jesus takes us back to the Father (John 14:6). In our union with Jesus, all the blessings which flow to the beloved one now also flow to us (Eph 1:3,6). And this union is not something we do; it is something which is done for us. "The most important thing about any one of us is not what we do but what God does, not what we do for God but what God does for us."[108] Before we were even born, God looked deep inside us, saw the wonder and the horror, and adopted us. He didn't wait for us to behave before he chose us. He chose us in spite of our behaviour and brought us into the intimacy and community of the Trinity (John 14:20). No longer do we look up and see the frowning eyes of a judge, we see the eyes of a father. No longer do we hear the harsh voice of a judge, we hear the warm voice of a father. He may discipline (Heb 12:6), but he is never harsh.

Imagine it is early in the morning at the Sondergeld house. My sons trundle into the kitchen for breakfast. As each of them gets his breakfast ready, it becomes apparent there is not enough honey to go around. One grabs the honey bottle and quickly squeezes the last of the honey on his breakfast before his brother can use it. An early morning scuffle breaks out and ends with both of them on the floor. My wife and I step in and break it up. Eventually, everything calms down and we sit down and talk about what has just happened. Imagine I said to them, "Right, because you two have sinned against each other and have ruined what should have been a peaceful breakfast for the rest of us, you are no longer my sons until your behaviour improves. Until further notice, you are out of the family." Who does that?! That's ridiculous, right? Yes, it is. If your family operates like that, then you need to know it is not normal. It's not the way it's supposed to be. Your position in the family is not based on behaviour, it is in a different category entirely. Good behaviour didn't get us into God's family and bad behaviour won't kick us out. Your position in the family is not in question. It is sure.

What you need to do is settle into your place in God's family. You need to live into who God has made you to be. You can stop playing the approval game and put the performance cue back in the rack. It never got you what you most deeply wanted and, in the light of what Jesus has done, it would be weird for you to use it again (Gal 3:3). Get involved in the family and let the family values rub off on you. This process will be easier for some than others. Expect your experiences from your biological family to colour the way you engage with God's family. To one degree or another, all our families leave marks on us, some physical and others non-physical. But the good news is that any effects from our biological families are trumped by being part of God's family. Our broken earthly families don't have the last word.

Spend time getting closer to the Father, enjoy communion with your brother Jesus (Heb 2:11) and marvel at the way the Spirit stirs you up to cry out "Abba, Father" (Rom 8:15).

> *For you did not receive the spirit of slavery to fall back into fear, but you have received the Spirit of adoption as sons, by whom we cry, "Abba! Father!" The Spirit himself bears witness with our spirit that we are children of God. (Rom 8:15–16)*

Scripture reading
Genesis 3, 1 Corinthians 4:1–5

For reflection and discussion

1. When have you tried to fix yourself up? How did it go?

2. How can you tell when your self is noisy?

3. What would it be/is it like to be comfortable in your own skin?

4. When do you switch to performance in an effort to deal with the noisiness in your self?

5. Whose approval do you live for?
   a. Your own
   b. Other people's
   c. God's

6. What does your approval system look like?
   a. What is the moral code? What are good and bad behaviours in your system?
   b. What do guilt and shame look like?
   c. What does the system of atonement look like? How do you get back to being righteous again?

7. When does despair show up in your efforts to live for the approval of others?

8. Our adoption into God's family disconnects our performance from our identity. How is this good news for you personally?

8. God's family – the place you become truly human

You can be anything you want to be.
You've probably heard this catchcry before. It often comes from the mouth of someone who has achieved an amazing feat. They stared their seemingly insurmountable goal in the face, they worked hard over a long period of time, and they ended up the victor. News cameras often capture the closing moments of their triumph and in the obligatory follow-up interview, with the adrenaline of success still pumping through their veins, they declare, "Don't give up. Chase your dreams. You can be anything you want to be." It is an unashamed appeal to you who are stuck, intimidated or suppressed, to break the shackles and go after what you really want. The impassioned declaration implies that the only thing in between the person you are and the person you want to be is commitment and hard work. And it resonates with many of us. We know what it is like to be stuck, or to hesitate in fear, or be limited by the expectations and stereotypes of others—and many of us secretly want to break free and be who we want to be. But you need to be careful with these kinds of motivational statements; the devil is in the details.

Like most maxims, this proclamation is both helpful and unhelpful. It is helpful in that it stirs us up to be something more than what our fears or other people's expectations make us. But it is also unhelpful because it simply isn't true. You can't be anything you want to be—sorry to burst your bubble. If you are five foot one, then you probably won't be playing in the NBA. If you struggled to understand basic mathematics, then you probably aren't going to be the lead engineer developing rockets for astronauts. Sure, there are exceptions. We can and do have hidden talents and abilities which are untapped due to fear, a lack of confidence, or cultural stereotypes. But regardless of these minor exceptions, this principle does not hold true. While there are some things we can do, there are also many things we can't. It's just the way it is.

Another significant problem with this maxim is that it assumes we are the masters of our own destinies. It declares that who we want to be is within arm's reach and it's up to us to reach out and take it. What is holding us back, what is in the way of us being truly great, is up to us—we just need to decide what we want and commit to achieving it. But be on your guard; while it may sound noble, it merely smuggles performance into our lives again, though under a different guise. Who we are and what we do become connected again. And while one moment of triumph might appear to be strong enough to anchor our identity, it won't be. It will never be enough. You will need another success, and then another one, and then…it's a trap.

Who we are is beyond us

The truth is, the choices which were made for us have a much greater influence on who we are than any choices we have made ourselves. We didn't decide what country we would be born in, who our family would be, what genes we would have, how affluent our parents would be, how many siblings we would have, what gender they would be, whether our parents would stay together, whether our parents would love us or abuse us. These massive, life-altering factors, along with countless more, were out of your control. You didn't have a say in them. Your choices are, at best, the garnish on the meal, not the meal itself. You could have been born in a refugee camp, to a father who was then killed in war and a mother who is numb from repetitive sexual assault. That would have had a massive effect on who you became.

We need to come to terms with the reality that who we are, and who we become, is mostly beyond our control. God decided where we would be born, who our parents would be, where we would live (Acts 17:26) and what we look like physically (Ps 139:13–14). He is the one who gives us "life and breath and everything" (Acts 17:25). Sometimes we protest about our lack of choice, especially when we are unhappy or we are struggling with our lot. And, in one sense, who could blame us? Life can be difficult and painful. But there is a better way forward than stomping our feet in displeasure and working to wrestle control back from God. Working with him is the way forward; it is the only way forward. I invite you to pay attention to him and what he is doing around you, with you and in you. It is bound to be good.

Despite everything that has happened to you, the most significant life-altering choice in your life was God's decision to adopt you into his family (Eph 1:5). This is at the top of the list. It may feel as though there are other contenders for the number one spot, but in reality, nothing else comes close. God's acceptance of you rewrites your past, energises your present and gives you unshakeable hope for eternity. It is more significant than swimming the English Channel, climbing Everest, or miraculously getting that functional family you long for. And you had no part in it. It was totally outside your control—and it was beautiful.

Adopted children are almost never the lead actors in their own adoptions; their adoptive parents are. Whilst it helps for an older child to agree to their adoption, almost all of the actions that matter in an adoption are done for the child, not by the child. This is true with us too. God saw us in our estranged state and got to work doing everything necessary to bring us back into his family. Adoption was God's way of ensuring that those who were banished did not remain outcasts (2 Sam 14:14). When you came to faith, the adoption which was arranged before the foundation of the world (Eph 1:4) was sealed. The orphan, the estranged child, had an instant family. You were far away, but you were brought near (Eph 2:13). He set his heart upon you and he will never change his mind.

Family hesitations

While all this talk of family may sound wonderful, for some people (perhaps even most) it sends a cold chill up their spine. If your family experience was difficult and painful then don't be surprised if this topic stirs up some unwanted emotions. There may be some who would prefer I didn't even use the word family. Your lived experience of family has resulted in a sharp dislocation between romantic ideals and harsh realities. Your family wasn't a good experience. As a child, you thought your experience was normal. You thought it was the way family was meant to work. But as you grew up, you spoke to more and more people and saw more and more clearly how messy your family actually was. Some of you only realised how problematic your family was after you were married; with the creation of a new family, the influences from your family of origin intersected with your spouse's in an up-close-and-personal way. It can be revelatory and tricky, often at the same time.

Families are messy because they are filled with messy people. For good or for ill, we all bring who we are into our family unit; familial messiness is directly connected to individual messiness. If there are angry people in the family who doggedly pursue their own agenda without any thought for others, then don't be surprised if screaming, shouting and physical abuse are close by. If there are people in the family who harbour unforgiveness and revenge, then don't be surprised if you see fragmentation, division, and taking sides. If there are people in the family who are committed conflict avoiders, or those desperate for the approval of others, then don't be surprised if you see a thin covering of superficial politeness with manipulation and control running just under the surface.

When you bring imperfect people together, messiness often multiplies. In a family, each person's messiness has a way of pressing other family members' buttons. Families are a mixture of those who seek approval and those who are harsh, those who are timid and those who are selfishly assertive, those who are careless with their words and those who are sensitive to the words of others. Individual messiness can take on a life of its own in the family. Some of you know what I am talking about. It isn't just that people were imperfect in your family; you had margin for that. It was what it ballooned into when they were together. The effect was much, much bigger than the sum of all those who lived under the one roof. So all this talk of joining another family, God's imperfect family, leaves you somewhere between hesitation and repulsion.

Sin has made every family dysfunctional in one way or another. Trace the effects of sin and you will find its most powerful work is reserved for what is most precious (family and sexuality for example). And once it is attached, it gets to work disordering and breaking the family unit down, swinging punches like a drunken man, hurting everyone as it goes.

God is well aware of the dysfunctionalities within families. If you go looking for a functional family in the Bible you will end up disappointed. There aren't many in there. While some of them get close to being harmonious, they are all dysfunctional in some way. Start at the beginning with Adam and Eve. You would think they would know how to do it, but they didn't do so well. By definition, if one of your children murders another one (Gen 4), you have some issues with your family culture! If you move onto Noah's family, things appear to be looking up. That is until Noah gets drunk, lies around naked and one of his sons laughs at him. The story ends in tears when Noah sobers up and pronounces a curse on his son (Gen 9:24–27). That would make for some pretty awkward family gatherings!

As you move further into Scripture, it doesn't get any better. You might think Abram, the father of many nations (Gen 17:5), would do better. But he doesn't. He takes the advice of his wife and has sex with their servant girl in an effort to have a son. When she conceives, his wife gets jealous and treats the servant girl harshly until she runs away (Gen 16). And we aren't even halfway through the book of Genesis! Move a little further into the Old Testament and you will discover Samuel's step-mum was a bully (1 Sam 1:6), and King David (the man after God's own heart) could run a country but not his own family. One of his sons raped his half-sister, David did nothing about it, and eventually one of her other brothers took matters into his own hands and murdered the one who raped her (2 Sam 13). You probably get the point by now. If you are looking for the perfect family in the Bible, you will be hard-pressed to find it.

But for all this talk about family dysfunction, we haven't addressed the elephant in the room—our own earthly fathers. For many of us, our hang-ups with our broader family fade into insignificance in comparison with the marks our fathers have left on us. Some of these are deeper and longer-lasting than any which came from the rest of our family. Follow the thread from your wounds back to your father and, more often than not, it will lead to some kind of abuse of power. He either used his power against his family or for himself or some mixture of the two. Maybe he was violent; he had an explosive temper and he would blow up at a moment's notice. Or maybe he was a sexual deviant; he had his go-to porn, and the way he looked at you was never right. Sometimes he even touched you in ways a child should never be touched and you can't get it out of your mind—you still feel dirty. For others, it wasn't that your dad did stuff to hurt you, he just never did anything. He was absent. When you needed him, he wasn't there—physically or emotionally. You could never talk with him about anything important because he was always somewhere else—at work, in the shed, in his head.

Despite these well-documented problems with family, it remains the main context that God uses to shape you into who he made you to be. He designed it this way in the very beginning. Your family of origin is the place he created for you to mature, grow up, and learn who you are. It is here you learn about what is important and how to relate to others.

Family design

Our family is the primary place where we learn how to interpret our world. We are interpreters by nature. "We do not live life based on the bare facts of our existence; we live our lives according to our interpretation of those facts."[109] In the beginning, humanity was part of God's family and God was the one who provided the framework through which his children were to interpret their world. His word was to be the lens through which they would understand and interpret themselves and the world around them. But God was not to be the only one forming the interpretive glasses of his children. Before long, Scripture records the delegation of this task to fathers, who become responsible for informing and shaping the interpretive glasses their children wear (Deut 6:7, Eph 6:4). Sadly, many fathers didn't and don't teach their children about God—but this doesn't mean their children are left without interpretive glasses. They are still given glasses by their parents, but these glasses are different, unclear, and sometimes harmful. Unfortunately for many, the proverb connecting training to their future behaviour rings true, for good or for ill: "Train up a child in the way he should go; even when he is old, he will not depart from it" (Prov 22:6).

Your family's values were the underpinning framework which informed the way you interpreted life. Your family values can be observed in what you and your siblings were disciplined for, what behaviours were rewarded, and what the family most frequently talked about. While your family's values have shaped much of who you are today, you probably didn't notice them most of the time.

They were the air you breathed, the environment you swam in. You didn't know any different—that is, until you left home and began living with other people. At that point, people probably began reacting to some of the strange things you did, and you began questioning your family's values.

In a family unit, family values are both taught and caught. As the most authoritative figures in the family unit, it is normally the parents' responsibility to teach whatever the family values are to their children. Whilst there ought to be a proactive component to this, children naturally learn the family values by following the example of their parents. Sometimes they will see what a parent is doing and knowingly copy it. Other times they will imitate their parents unknowingly. And actions speak louder than words—when a parent's instruction and their life don't match, the child inevitably follows what the parent does, rather than what they say. A family's values are the air the family breathes.

If your biological family was difficult and the thought of being in another one troubles you, then there is hope for you. Your own family was never meant to be the ultimate expression of family. It was only ever meant to be a subset of God's family—all fatherhood comes from him (Eph 3:15). This is why the psalmist can say, "My father and my mother have forsaken me, but the LORD will take me in" (Ps 27:10). It is also why Jesus calls upon us to prioritise our allegiance to him over our allegiance to our biological families (Luke 14:26). So it is a relief to learn that all is not lost when biological families break down. Not even close. The most significant family on the face of the planet is God's family. It is the one which exerts the most influence on you. Your biological family may have left significant marks on you, but it doesn't have the last word. God does.

Family likeness

As you work your way through the New Testament, you might notice a curious and rather silent transition taking place. In the gospels, the category of discipleship is very prominent. Jesus speaks of it regularly and he sets a high bar for anyone contemplating becoming his disciple (Matt 16:24). But as we move away from the gospels, the discipleship category begins to fade out. In fact, Acts 21:16 is the last reference to discipleship in the New Testament. It never gets another mention. In its place, familial categories such as Father (Rom 8:14–15), son (Gal 3:26), brother and sister (1 Cor 1:10, Rom 16:1) become much more prominent.

Why the category shift from discipleship to family? It appears the writers in the early church absorbed the category of discipleship into the much larger category of family. Discipleship didn't end, but it became part of something much bigger and much more significant. No longer are we merely disciples emulating our teacher. We are much closer than that. We are members of a family now. We are in a household (Eph 2:19). We are children learning to live more deeply into our God-given identity.[110]

In God's family, it is normal to imitate your heavenly Father. "Therefore, be imitators of God, as beloved children" (Eph 5:1). He is a loving father and you are beloved children. He is the definer of what is good and right and important in his family. You can trust him. You don't always need to know why something is good; if God said it is good, then it must be. Your task is not to doubt him or take over from him. Your task is to abide in him, imitate him, and settle into your place in his family. "Little children, abide in him, so that when he appears we may have confidence and not shrink from him in shame at his coming. If you know that he is righteous, you may be sure that everyone who practices righteousness has been born of him" (1 John 2:28–29). It is our resemblance to the Father that proves we are legitimate children.[111]

Like any family, God sets the example and teaches his children the family values (Rom 8:13–14). It is the child's responsibility to imitate their father and take on the family likeness. "No one born of God makes a practice of sinning, for God's seed abides in him; and he cannot keep on sinning, because he has been born of God.

By this it is evident who are the children of God" (1 John 3:9–10). This family likeness ought to be discernible from one child to the next, but it isn't sameness. God has not called us to be clones of one another. We are to bear the family likeness inside our own skin.

Although there are many ways in which we need to take on the family likeness, let us look briefly at four key areas which make a direct contribution to who we are and how we can operate humanly. Some of these concern our imitation of God, and others are concerned with how we operate rightly in relation to God.

In God's family, we settle into our finiteness

In God's family, he is infinite, we are not. We are dependent. We see the evidence of this in the opening chapter of Scripture. Even though Adam and Eve were "perfect people living in perfect relationship with him, they could not figure out life on their own."[112] They needed God's revelation to know who they were and what they were to do (Gen 1:28–30). They also needed each other (Gen 1:27, 2:18). These realities were well established before sin entered the world. We have limits. We are not self-contained. We are not self-sustaining. If you put a human in a sealed box and left them there, they would die; if you could put God inside a sealed box, he would live forever.

The thought of our reliance upon God and others feels unnatural for us. It runs in the opposite direction to the proud independence which lit up Adam and Eve's heart and continues in our own. Our hearts still resonate with the words of Ralph Waldo Emerson, "Self-trust is the first secret of success."[113] But it is a trick. It is a lie. In God's family, independence is not an ingredient for success—dependence is. Rather than pushing against dependence, you ought to embrace it, settle into it, and enjoy it. It will bring peace and strength to your soul (Isa 30:15).

In God's family, independent strength is shameful and dependent weakness is honourable. This is the exact opposite of what we often think. Sin always pushes us away from how God originally made us to operate. The apostle Paul knew what it was like to have people pushing him away from how God had made him to operate. In 2 Corinthians 12, Paul is partway through responding to people who were critical of how he presented and the way he spoke (2 Cor 10:10). In their world, oratory prowess and physical strength were honourable, and weakness was shameful. But they had it wrong, and Paul let them know. In God's family, weak dependence is honourable and self-sufficiency is shameful. Paul knew it because Jesus had told him, "'My grace is sufficient for you, for my power is made perfect in weakness.' Therefore, I will boast all the more gladly of my weaknesses, so that the power of Christ may rest upon me" (2 Cor 12:9). Jesus was helping Paul return to normal human operation.

Boasting in our weakness is not about glorifying our weaknesses; it is about clear and direct admission of our limitations in the light of God's resourcing and strength. We boast in our weakness when we are honest about what we are not good at, or the troubles we are facing, or the personal flaw which regularly gets the better of us. Boasting in our weakness is impossible if we continue to restlessly snatch after strength or greatness. It will only be a feature of our lives when we are settled into our finiteness, our dependence on God. At the start, this attitude may feel a little ill-fitting, but don't give up; before long it will fit you like a glove.

What would it look like if God's family settled into their finiteness? It looks like …

> … not needing to know everything. When someone comes up to you and they have an idea you didn't think of, you don't feel bad about it, because you aren't God and you don't know everything. Expect people to have ideas that you don't. Instead, think, "Of course they would think of something I didn't. I don't know everything. I should expect people to tell me things I don't know regularly. That's exactly what I need."

… speedy, clear admissions when you get something wrong. Start with the expectation that you will get things wrong; for one thing, you don't know everything, and for another, you are a sinner. Start the day expecting you will need to say sorry for something during the day. It is bound to happen. In God's family, you don't have to pretend you have it all together. No one does. And if it looks like others have it all together, don't believe it.

… learning how to fail. Track back for a moment and revisit the systems of approval from the last chapter. You might have noticed none of them have an effective system of atonement. When you boil it down, none of them have a way back from failure. The result of this is if you live for approval too long, you will forget how to fail. It isn't that you won't fail—failure is a certainty. It's that you can't allow yourself to, so when you do, you won't be able to admit, accept, or live with it. But when you realise you are finite and fallen, you can relax a little bit.

… not needing to be good at everything. God has given people different gifts and talents. No one has them all (1 Cor 12:29–30). It's okay to be really lousy at some things. Sometimes, in our efforts to be the complete package, we try to excel at something we are not particularly gifted in. Whilst we may see some marginal improvement, trying to be strong in areas where we are not gifted only tends to end in frustration and a loss of confidence. A well-rounded expression of gifts and talents is found in a whole community, not an individual.

Beware of the way other people's expectations can prevent you from settling into your finiteness. Paul understood this. He knew the expectations other people had of him and the temptation to live for the approval of others was real. He could have attempted some super-human feat, or sought out help from one of the great orators of the day, or begun working out in the gym. But he didn't. His thorn in the flesh, his perennial weakness, kept him grounded in who he was and who God was. People will often expect you to know more, be in more places, and be able to do more things than you were made to do. They will expect you to have superhuman abilities and will reward you with praise if they think they see some. Make sure you remind them of your limitations, of what you can and can't do, and be prepared to deal with their disappointment in you from time to time.

In God's family, everyone is unfinished

In my time as a pastor and counsellor, I have had the great privilege of hearing many people's personal stories. Most of the time they share because they are struggling and their story helps to decode a little of what is going on for them. In the early days, some of their stories surprised me. Not so much because of the content, but because of the person who was telling me the story. They seemed so…squeaky clean, together, under control. The way they presented didn't seem to match up with the messiness of their backstory. But before long, the penny dropped. I realised everyone has a backstory, even—perhaps especially—those who appear to have it all together. I once thought there were two different categories of people in the church: those who had it together and those who didn't. Now I realise there is only one—those who don't have it all together.

Jesus' priority is to walk with you, not fix you. He knows your 'fixing' is downstream of intimate relationship with you. He knows your restoration won't be finished until the day he comes (Phil 1:6) and he is okay with that. You can relax. While he will be persistent in changing you, you can expect the process to be mixed with lashings of patience. While he could turn up next to your bed at seven o'clock in the morning and read out a thousand things you need to get sorted out by morning tea, he doesn't. "He knows our frame; he remembers that we are dust" (Ps 103:14). He has compassion for his children (Ps 103:13). He knows you get overloaded quickly and you can't deal with too many things at once. He has a comprehensive restoration plan for you. Expect his restorative work to be deep, well-planned, incremental, and methodical.

When we own the reality that everyone is messy and unfinished, we will be able to resist the urge to fix others too. Our tendency to want to fix others is often a combination of our discomfort at what they have shared, an overestimation of our own abilities, and an assumption that the seat of their problem is their behaviour. The prophet Jeremiah had a far more sobering take on the nature of sin and the extent of human abilities: "The heart is deceitful above all things, and desperately sick; who can understand it? 'I the Lord search the heart and test the mind'" (Jer 17:9–10). While we can see and identify errant behaviour, we don't understand the internal machinations of our own hearts, let alone anyone else's. And if we don't understand the true nature of the problem, how could we ever fix anyone? We are not change agents. At best we are catalysts. While God may use us to contribute to the context for change, he is the one who does the changing.

When God called me and my wife to plant a church ten years ago, he led a wise old Christian man to join the church and support us. His name was John. Our church-planting team was quite young and we highly valued John's wisdom and deep relationship with Jesus. He joined the church midway through a particularly difficult season of his life. Over a fourteen-year period he had: broken his back falling from a ladder, a brain haemorrhage, heart bypass surgery, died on an operating table, a dozen tumours develop throughout his body. A couple of months before he died, I dropped in to see him at his house. At one point in the conversation, he leaned forward and said, "God woke me up the other night Peter, and he showed me there is still some brass in my heart which he wants to deal with." What he meant was there was a part of his heart which still needed to change. He was 73 and close to death, and God was still changing him.

As more and more of God's children embody the family likeness, expect things in his family to get messier. So brace yourself. If you want to live out this family's values, your neat church will get messier. It won't lead to more sin, but it will lead to more people talking about sin, and it will provide the space for sinners to be authentically fallen. Sordid stories will come from those you least expect. Others will watch for a while and take notes on how people are handled before they start talking about the mess in their lives. It will get messier, but it will be good, I assure you. And remember, there is actually no such thing as a neat church and a messy church, only those churches who talk about their mess and those who don't.

For some, all this talk about being unfinished leaves you throwing up your hands in despair. You might be thinking, "What's the point of trying if I am never going to make it, if I'm always going to be unfinished? I give up." I want to encourage you, don't give up. Your restoration will lead to freedom, love, wholeness and peace. Get as much of it as you can. My friend Mark is. He came to me a while ago asking to be baptised. I sat down with Mark and his wife to talk about his backstory and where his desire to be baptised was coming from. It was a riveting tale. As a child, his father taught him to stand up for himself. In adulthood, he served as an intelligence officer in the South African armed forces. He also occupied a leadership role in a prominent motorcycle club. He said to me, "Sex and drugs weren't really my thing. Violence was my thing." I believed him. He was built like a tank. He talked about how Jesus had come into his life and how he started changing. But although he had always had a place for God in his life, Mark had never submitted to him. Then the moment arrived where he decided to give his life over to Jesus and submit to him. Things really began to change. He turned, looked at his wife and said, "I haven't had an angry outburst for eight years." She nodded and said to me, "It's true. He hasn't." It was a big deal. I momentarily paused and thought, "That is so beautiful and so good." Jesus was changing him for the better, and it was good for everyone—including him.

Your restoration is already underway. Jesus is at work in you right now. You aren't the same today as you were a year ago. He is growing and maturing you. And he will work on those stubbornly immature bits, sooner or later. You can be sure of that. So reach out for everything he has for you. Your complete restoration is assured. "I am sure of this, that he who began a good work in you will bring it to completion at the day of Jesus Christ" (Phil 1:6).

In God's family, we interrupt each other's shame

If it is to be a powerfully restorative culture, God's family needs to be particularly attentive to the presence of shame. In any group culture, the power of shame is normally proportional to the clarity of the group's moral code. The clearer the moral code in a group, the greater the power of shame. Look at the church. We have one of the clearest moral codes going around. We all have a copy of it (the Bible), and most of us can pick out bad behaviour at a hundred yards. This reality alone leaves the church susceptible to becoming a caustically powerful shame culture. When shame takes over, it eats away the church's mission from the inside out, leaving only a shell on the outside. It relationally isolates people and interrupts the restorative dynamic of knowing and being known. Shame is public enemy number one for the local church.

In God's family, we interrupt shame by recognising we all have a similar disorder. Wherever shame is present, you will find a pecking order. There are little sinners and there are big sinners. To be a good person in a shame culture, you need to avoid becoming a big sinner and avoid associating with big sinners. But God ranks people based on what is going on in their hearts (the non-physical part of the person comprising the mind, will and emotions), and the news is not good. All of our evil behaviour flows out of our hearts (Matt 15:18–19). All of our sin, no matter what it is, boils down to this: relational unfaithfulness. God doesn't tell us some are sick and some aren't; he says we are all sick. Some worship work, others alcohol, some worship their achievements, and others the highs of sex or illicit drugs, but there is no pecking order. While the expression of our hearts may differ from person to person, underneath we are more like each other than unlike each other.[114]

In God's family, we interrupt shame by drawing close to the shame-filled person. Shame won't be dispelled by lobbing Scripture grenades or merely telling someone we love them from a distance. Shame is stubborn. It won't surrender to any remote attack. It needs to be dealt with in hand-to-hand combat. It needs our personal engagement. There is no other way. If we want to see shame interrupted then we will need to love one another the way God has loved us (John 13:34). How did God love us? He came close to sinners, those who had failed. "Christ Jesus came into the world to save sinners—of whom I am the worst" (1 Tim 1:15).[115] This is classic Jesus. He seemed to have a fondness for being close to big sinners, so much so that some of their reputation rubbed off on him. He was called the "friend of sinners" (Matt 11:19) by some of his opponents. It wasn't a compliment. But for the shame-filled, there is no more sublime statement. A friend is just what they need, someone who will interrupt their shame-fuelled isolation by coming close.

In God's family, we interrupt shame with a mixture of truth and personal presence. If you want to help the shame-filled, you will need to spend time with them and learn how shame operates in their life. Be on the lookout for their shame tells—listen carefully when they apologise for things they shouldn't, take notice when they downplay or discount something they have done, pay attention when they pull away from relational engagement with others. Be a good listener; people almost always talk and share more with a good listener. And always be prepared to invite them to share more of their story with you. If they talk about a time when they reacted in a certain way, ask them what was going on in that moment. Your task is a little like the computer expert in the classic Hollywood 'alien invasion' movie plotline: your objective is to hack into their shame operating system and upload some computer code which will blow the system up. And there is nothing more powerful in breaking down shame in others than being with them, knowing them at their worst, and speaking deep gracious truth to them:

> I see you. I know you. I am with you.
>
> You belong to him. You are his child.
>
> He knows you fully and loves you fully.
>
> He is with you right now. He does not hesitate to associate with you.

The combination of truth and personal presence won't compute with their shame and walls will start falling down. Nothing is more powerful.

In God's family, we rehearse identity with each other

When my children were younger, my wife and I sent them to vacation care during the school holidays. Our boys normally enjoyed going to vacation care, but there was one day which was an exception. On this particular day, a new staff member took a dislike to one of my boys and was harsh in the way she handled him, using expletives and a rather gruff manner to get him to do what she wanted him to. His brothers noticed what was happening and knew something was not right. They responded by pulling in tight with their brother and supporting him for the remainder of the day. They weren't arrogant or disrespectful to the woman, but they did stand with their brother against her unprofessional behaviour.

At dinner time, we sat together and shared the stories of the day. The three boys who went to vacation care talked about the woman, what she had done, and how they had responded. As they shared the story of their day, I was proud of them. They had done exactly what I had taught them to do. While I had taught them to be respectful, I had also taught them that Sondergelds back one another. This is what we do. This is who we are. Sure, there are fights and quarrels between the brothers from time to time, but when one Sondergeld is under attack, we close ranks and support one another. At the end of our dinner conversation, I rehearsed identity with my family. I reminded them, "Sondergelds back one another. We aren't rude or disrespectful, but when someone is up to no good and one of us is under attack, we all are. We don't abandon them. Sondergelds have each other's back."

The apostle Peter does something similar to this in 2 Peter 1. In this section, Peter is encouraging Christians to take on the family likeness of virtue, knowledge, self-control, steadfastness, godliness, brotherly affection, and love (2 Pet 1:5–7). Then he tells them the reason why these qualities may be lacking. "For whoever lacks these qualities is so nearsighted that he is blind, having forgotten that he was cleansed from his former sins" (2 Pet 1:9). They had forgotten who they were, so Peter reminded them (and us).

If you read on a little more, it will help you to get an aerial view of what Peter is up to.

> Therefore, brothers, be all the more diligent to confirm your calling and election, for if you practice these qualities you will never fall ... Therefore I intend always to remind you of these qualities, though you know them and are established in the truth that you have. I think it right ... to stir you up by way of reminder ... And I will make every effort so that after my departure you may be able at any time to recall these things. (2 Pet 1:10,12–13,15)

Peter is delivering a family exhortation. Sure, they are the words of someone inspired to write Holy Scripture, but notice the second word in this section: "brothers". Then, in verses 12–15, Peter talks about the ongoing, repeated commitment he is making to his family members to remind them of who they are in Jesus. This is a family talk. A family talk about who we are, which was inspired by the Father, through a brother. God's family is meant to operate a little like the talk at the Sondergeld table. We are family and so we talk about what happens to members of the family. We talk about who the family is, what the family does, and how the family acts. We rehearse our identity with each other.

Most of the time, family identity is unseen. We don't think about it and we don't talk about it much, at least not explicitly. But I think we could talk about it a little more. We could rehearse identity with one another more explicitly. It won't take much more effort, but it will require us to be more intentional about paying attention to those living out of a false identity, and leaning in with an encouraging reminder. Here are a few identity statements to get you started:

> We are not slaves to fear. We are powerful.
>
> We are not victims, we are conquerors.
>
> We get up when we are knocked down.
>
> We are okay with not knowing the future.
>
> We know there will always be enough grace for every moment.
>
> We know, whatever situation we find ourselves in, God will come for us.

When family goes wrong

I wish I didn't have to add this section. I wish I could say, "All you need to do is jump into God's family and you will receive all the help you need." But it doesn't always work that way. Allow me to back up for a moment. Who has God adopted into his family? Imperfect sinners. When is he going to finish the work he has begun in them? On the day when Jesus returns. Can you see any potential problems? What could possibly go wrong?

Sometimes people outside of our church ask me, "How is the church going?" My typical answer is, "Well, the church is full of sinners and is led by sinners, so it has its complications. But in spite of that, it is going pretty well." Let's be honest—at its best, the church is a pretty ramshackle organisation. While it is powerful for good, it can be powerful for ill too. Help and hurt come through the same pipe. The church is about relationships and, in a fallen world, both help and hurt always come to us through the pipeline of relationships.

Troubles in churches happen wherever incomplete saints are. We all take our personal baggage with us wherever we go. It saddens me to say, but there will be times in the church when the sheep will bite each other, and times when church leaders (Jesus' under-shepherds) will feed on the sheep, rather than feeding the sheep (Ezek 34:3). It can be a real mess. Some of you know what I am talking about. There are pieces of you that are missing. God's family brought some healing but it also inflicted some wounds. You have both the healing and the scars to prove it. What are we to do?

Some choose to opt out. They have decided there is no net gain from the church and have disengaged. In many ways, I understand where they are coming from. There is a logic to it. But when it comes to God's plans and purposes, there is no plan B. The church is it. This is the place God has designed for us to grow to maturity (Eph 4:12–13), and it is the gathering which will storm the gates of hell (Matt 16:18). The church is amazing, scary, incredible, and sometimes painful. Expect to see each of these aspects in one way or another. (However, if your church is perpetually toxic, then it may be time to leave it and find one with a more restorative culture. They are out there.)

The church, the gathering of God's people, is the place where God has determined you will be restored. And you will be restored, even if it hurts you. God will see to it that every wound ends up glorious. You see, it isn't the structure or the people in the church that make it restorative; it is God's presence within it. After all, it is his temple (Eph 2:21).

For thus says the Lord GOD: Behold, I, I myself will search for my sheep and will seek them out. As a shepherd seeks out his flock when he is among his sheep that have been scattered, so will I seek out my sheep, and I will rescue them from all places where they have been scattered ... I will bring them out from the peoples and gather them from the countries, and will bring them into their own land ... I will feed them with good pasture, and ... they shall lie down in good grazing land, and on rich pasture ... I myself will be the shepherd of my sheep, and I myself will make them lie down ... I will seek the lost, and I will bring back the strayed, and I will bind up the injured, and I will strengthen the weak, and the fat and the strong I will destroy. (Ezek 34:11–16)

Scripture reading
2 Corinthians 10–12, 2 Peter 1

For reflection and discussion

1. How comfortable are you with the thought that most of who you are is beyond your control?

2. How content are you with the way God has made you? Do you think he did a good job?

3. How has your biological family shaped you for good? How have they shaped you for ill?

4. Which parts of the way you interpret life stem from your biological family? Which bits would you like God to rewrite?

5. Which of God's family values comes most easily to you? Which one do you find the most challenging? Why?
    a. We settle into our finiteness
    b. We are unfinished
    c. We interrupt each other's shame
    d. We rehearse identity with each other

6. Which of the following evidences of settling into your finiteness would you like to grow in?
    a. Not needing to know everything
    b. Speedy, clear admissions when you are wrong
    c. Learning how to fail
    d. Not needing to be good at everything

7. Who rehearses your identity with you? What do they say?

8. At what times and in what places do you most need to rehearse your God-given identity? What can/do you say to yourself?

9. Becoming you

Some years ago, I was helping out a couple who were struggling in their marriage. The husband was a very strong man. He always knew what he wanted and he didn't hesitate in saying what he thought. His wife, on the other hand, was almost the complete opposite. She was quieter and much more reserved than he, and she organised her life around doing whatever it took to please him. In some ways, it was the perfect arrangement. One was strong and the other wasn't. One was clear about what they wanted and the other was committed to giving them what they wanted. It was a perfect business arrangement, but a struggling relationship. In the wife's effort to please her husband, she had completely disappeared. She was physically present but personally invisible, and her invisibility made a genuine relationship between them impossible. And who could blame her? Even if she wanted to be personally present, there wasn't really any space for her. If they were going to have a good, healthy relationship, she would need to become more personally present and he would need to make space for her. Would it be easy? Probably not. But it was the only way forward.

True humans and being personally present

Prior to the fall, Adam and Eve were always personally present.

"The man and his wife were both naked and were not ashamed" (Gen 2:25). And why would they be? They were truly human, imagers of God. They reflected his glory. There was no guilt, no shame, and nothing about them which was cringeworthy. But the onset of sin changed all that. Those who were once truly human, naked and not ashamed, were dehumanised. Parts of them were damaged, parts went missing, and hiding became one of their iconic moves. The erratic nature of humanity's personal presence became an ongoing sign of their dehumanisation. We go invisible whenever our humanity is corrupted by sin, damaged by others, or blocked by suffering. Or to put it another way:

> We go invisible when we act less than human, when we are treated as less than human, and when we are being prevented from being human.

Invisibility is about dehumanisation. Whenever our humanity is damaged, part of us is rubbed out. And while it doesn't change the objective truth about who we are (children and imagers of God), it does change the way we operate and the way others relate to us. In short, we end up living with a dehumanised identity, a dehumanised version of who we were created to be. We accept what our lusts, sin, shame and suffering say about us. We end up settling into shadows of our true selves. We need help to become truly human again.

Jesus, the true human, has acted decisively to restore us. But the job isn't finished yet—and he doesn't intend to complete it on his own (Eph 4:12). You can expect him to work directly with you and through your spiritual brothers and sisters. God has determined that his family will be the place where you will become your true self. He still sees the you who is "fearfully and wonderfully made" (Ps 139:14), and he plans on calling that person out. So, he does what any good father does; he leads by example and calls his children to imitate him (Eph 5:1).

"The God who sees me"

To all those who have lost touch with who God made them to be, God says, "I see you." But not in a hide and seek way. He doesn't say it because he has caught you out. He sees you in a deeply personal way. He sees the real you, the you he had in his mind's eye when he created you. When God kicked humanity out of the garden, he followed us out and kept an eye on us. He didn't watch us from a distance, he stayed close by. When all the ravages of this fallen world have done their dastardly work on you and you have gone invisible, he sees you.

One of the most beautiful pictures of God seeing humanity, and the effect of this on personal presence is found in Genesis 16. In the previous chapter, God had told Abram he would have offspring as numerous as the stars in the sky (Gen 15:5). This seemed unlikely to Abram because he and his wife Sarai had not been able to have children (Gen 15:3). He talked to God about this problem and God responded by promising him a son of his own (Gen 15:4).

Despite God's promise, by Genesis 16, we see that Abram and Sarai's childlessness was clearly getting to them. If Abram was to have offspring as numerous as the stars, he would need to have a son. There was no other way. But rather than wait for God, Sarai came up with a fix for the problem. After all, they weren't getting any younger. Sarai suggested to Abram that he sleep with their Egyptian servant, Hagar, in the hope she would bear him a son. They actioned the plan and Hagar conceived. Shortly afterwards, relational difficulties developed between the two women and Sarai wanted Abram to sort it out. He essentially wrote Sarai a blank cheque and said, "'Behold, your servant is in your power; do to her as you please.' Then Sarai dealt harshly with her, and she fled from her" (Gen 16:6).

What a sad story. We have only just moved out of the lofty heights of God's promises to Abram in Genesis 15 and are now in the pits. Does it remind you of anything? Did you notice any similarities between this episode and the fall of humanity? Theologians have.[116] Each of the words and key expressions of Genesis 16:2–3 finds a direct parallel in the fall of humanity back in Genesis 3.[117] While the practice of having children with servants was not uncommon in that day, the author of Genesis wants you to know something bad has happened. In reality, Genesis 16 chronicles another fall just like the first one,[118] with the same DNA and the same consequence. Note the parallel phrasing in the different accounts:

16:2	Sarai said to Abram	3:2	the woman said to the serpent
16:2	Abram listened to the voice of Sarai	3:17	you … listened to the voice of your wife
16:3	Sarai … took	3:6	she took
16:3	and gave her to Abram	3:6	she also gave some to her husband[119]

God had promised something good, something miraculous to Abram and Sarai, but they needed to wait for it. And, just like in the fall of humanity, they couldn't wait and they grasped for what God had promised to give them anyway. The destination was right, but their methodology was wrong because it depended on human effort rather than God's (Gal 4:23).

Under Sarai's harsh treatment, Hagar ran away (Gen 16:7). It was all too much. Sin and suffering, the usual suspects, had claimed another victim. Hagar ended up cutting a rather forlorn figure, alone and pregnant by a spring of water in the desert. Isolation and personal invisibility are partners in crime, two sides of the same coin. Once, Hagar was part of something, she had her place. But now she was in the middle of nowhere. Whether the situation was her fault or not is irrelevant. Like Adam and Eve, she had been exiled. Sin always drives people into the wilderness. It's either you or those around you. Someone has to go.

But God was watching. He could see Hagar. She wasn't lost to him. An angel of the Lord (God himself[120]) found her and engaged in what started as a pretty normal conversation with her: "Where did you come from?" and "Where are you going?" were his opening questions (Gen 16:7–8). Then he told her what he wanted her to do, before finishing up with some full-blown encouragement: he told her she was pregnant with a son through whom she would have countless descendants (Gen 16:10), and he made a point of letting her know he had heard her troubles (Gen 16:11). Indeed, this is the very meaning of Ishmael, the name God told her to call her son—*God hears*.

Hagar, like everyone else in the story, wasn't perfect. She appeared to have caused some of the trouble she was in and was also the recipient of some harsh treatment (she likely would have faced some more when she returned to Sarai, as the angel had instructed her). But things were different now. God had listened to her troubles (Gen 16:11). He had *seen* her. He had his eye on her. After the angel of the Lord left, Hagar did something no one else did in the whole of the Old Testament—she named God. And her choice of name is arresting. "So she called the name of the Lord who spoke to her, 'You are a God who sees me,' for she said, 'Truly here I have seen him who looks after me'" (Gen 16:13). He did see her. She wasn't invisible to him.

When God tells you he sees and hears you, what he is really saying is that he loves you. And the effect of his love is that we come out of the shadows. It draws us out. It makes us sit taller. It lifts our heads. It re-humanises us and makes us more visible. God's loving encouragement of Hagar ended in her heading home and taking her place under Sarai again. While some may wonder how she could do that, the answer is simple: God's love for people is so powerful it can enable them to be personally present in some of the most caustic places. When the great one notices you and loves you, it really means something.

The God who sees you

The way God saw and heard Hagar was a mere shadow compared

to the way God saw and heard humanity in the person of Jesus. In Jesus, God took on human flesh and physically looked into our eyes and heard our voices. He didn't gloss over people or hurry them along because there was a bigger crowd or a more important event he needed to get to. He gave them his personal attention, over and over again; "Now when the sun was setting, all those who had any who were sick with various diseases brought them to him, and he laid his hands on every one of them and healed them" (Luke 4:40). Jesus didn't restore people remotely, and he rarely performed group healings. There was something about Jesus' personal attention which made people more visible, something which made them more human.

Jesus doesn't just see us where we are at, he calls us out of the shadows. Remember the shame-filled woman who had been bleeding for twelve years? In the midst of a pressing crowd, Jesus felt some power go out from him, so he stopped and asked those around him, "Who was it that touched me?" (Luke 8:45–46) It was a ridiculous question to some. But it made all sorts of sense. He knew what had happened. The bleeding woman had stolen her healing by sneaking through the crowd and touching his robe. But Jesus was calling her out. Would she come out of hiding so Jesus could see her? In the end, she didn't have any choice. When she realised "she was not hidden" she fell "down before him ... And he said to her, 'Daughter, your faith has made you well; go in peace'" (Luke 8:47–48). In a moment she was healed of the physical sickness that had dogged her for so long. But this wasn't the best part of the healing. The best part of the healing was being seen by Jesus. That is what she needed most. She wasn't lost in a sea of faces. Her shame and the crowd couldn't hide her from his gaze. She wasn't invisible to him.

As Jesus died on the cross, God said definitively, once for all, "I see you. I see your sin, your shame, the grief you feel, and the sorrows you carry. I see you at your worst. I see you when you can't even bear to look at yourself. And I love you." As Jesus died, the hopes of all those who have been dehumanised and rubbed out by sin came alive. You see, Jesus didn't bear nondescript sins on the cross. He bore yours and mine (1 Pet 2:24). Every. Single. One. He didn't merely die for humanity in a general sense, he died for you and me. It was personal. No one got lost in the wash.

How God calls the real us out

God not only sees you in your dehumanised state, he can also see you in your rehumanised state. He knows how you have been made, and where sin has affected you, better than anyone else. And he is intent on reversing the curse and making you new again. The first step in this process was done for us by Jesus—he adopted us and united us to himself. The next step involves us becoming the person God has made us to be. This process is not one which only takes place within the confines of our relationship with God, it is one in which God's family plays a key part—we call out the person God made each of us to be.

The early days of King Saul provide a helpful picture of what I mean by 'calling someone out'. God's people disobediently demanded to have a king like all the nations around them (1 Sam 8). God rebuked them for it, but eventually granted their request and directed Samuel to anoint Saul as king (1 Sam 9). When Samuel found Saul, he waited until they were alone before anointing him (1 Sam 10), and Saul didn't tell a soul (1 Sam 10:16). Eventually, the time arrived for Saul to be publicly proclaimed as king but, when the big moment came, he was nowhere to be seen. So they asked God where Saul was and he tells them as only God can, "Behold, he has hidden himself among the baggage" (1 Sam 10:22). Then "they ran and took him from there" and "he stood among the people" (1 Sam 10:23). Saul was fearful; he couldn't see himself doing what God had called him to do. He needed other people to find him in the baggage and help him take his place. This picture captures some of the dynamic of calling someone out. We find those who are 'hidden in their own baggage' and help them become who God has made them to be in the place he has called them to.

Perhaps the idea of calling someone out sounds a little harsh to you. It may be because the most common use of the phrase in our culture has to do with drawing attention to someone's unacceptable behaviour. But that is not what I mean by the term. What I mean is this:

> We call someone out when we see something of who God made them to be and lovingly stir it up, so they grow more fully into who God had in his mind's eye when he created them.

You might prefer the term 'drawing out' to describe what I am talking about, but I think 'drawing someone out' is too passive. It doesn't capture the 'stirring up' nature of our task. The book of Hebrews captures some of the dynamic of stirring one another up—"Let us consider how to stir up one another to love and good works" (Heb 10:24). The stirring up of one another in this verse is not mainly about providing the opportunity for someone to do something good and then waiting for them to take it up. It is about actively calling people out; finding ways to incite and provoke good works in others. This is the way God talks to us, and it is the way we should be talking to one another.

Encouragement and calling people out

God mainly calls us out through encouragement. To encourage someone is to put courage into them. This is what God did to Hagar. He saw her in her troubles, came alongside her, and encouraged her. And we shouldn't be surprised by this; he is the God of all encouragement (Rom 15:5). What was the effect? Hagar was able to endure. What you see in this story can be seen in almost every good story—endurance and encouragement, running side by side. Throughout the Scriptures, God's people run into obstacles, encounter fears, get stuck in difficulty, and get tired. Over and over

God responds with encouragement. *I will help you. I will save you. I will turn everything to good. I will forgive you. I will be with you.* Encouragement. Over and over. He lays it on thick. He is "the God of endurance and encouragement" (Rom 15:5) and boy do we need it.

Before we move on and look at some practical ways we can encourage people, let's consider some of the basic elements of encouragement.

1. Encouragement always stirs people to action. It isn't merely nice words, it's a force that propels people forward. It puts ballast in their souls and stirs them to move towards what they fear, or the obstacle in their way. Deep encouragement always leads to resilience, determination, and the ability to endure what God has called a person to. It is essential for God's people to do the good works he has prepared for them.

2. Encouraging words have staying power. They are more like a three-course meal than a sugar hit. There are plenty of good things we can say that will give people a 'shot in the arm', but encouragement has a longer-term goal in mind. Well-timed encouragements are like good carbohydrates, which digest slowly and provide sustenance over the long term. They keep working long after they have been spoken.

3. Encouragement aligns well with the way we have been made. We are imagers by nature. We are designed to reflect something great. We are, by nature, distributors of God's greatness, not reservoirs of it. Encouragement highlights other people's connection to God and how he wants to use their gifts for his kingdom. "You have an amazing gift. You should keep using it."

4. Encouragement requires proximity. You have to be close to encourage others. While there are many things we can say from a distance which will bless people, if you want to encourage others then you need to be close enough to know their fears

and their challenges. The flip side is true too; if we don't allow ourselves to be known by others, then deep encouragement will be far less likely.

5. Encouragement is intentional. You have to lean in. Opportunities for encouragement abound, but you have to be ready for them; sit back and wait, and they will pass you by. But don't let it become mechanistic or you will turn other people into projects. You are not an expert and they are not your project; you are brothers and sisters, called to back your family. Encouragement is less about what you do, and more about who you are.

If you want to see a great example of calling someone out through encouragement, then you can't go past the apostle Paul with Timothy. While many have spent time studying the details of what Paul writes, we will spend the remainder of the chapter zooming out a little and considering what Paul is up to. Paul was close to Timothy. He was fiercely committed to Timothy being everything God had created him to be, in the place God had put him. The way he calls Timothy out provides some helpful guiding principles for how we can call one another out.

Paul and Timothy—a model for calling out

Timothy was the child of a mixed marriage, with a Jewish mother and a Greek father (Acts 16:1). His mother Lois and his grandmother Eunice were both devout Christians (2 Tim 1:5). He likely came to faith as a result of Paul's first missionary journey.[121] Before long, he became one of Paul's travelling companions (Acts 16:3), accompanying him on many journeys. He was young (1 Tim 4:12), tender-hearted (2 Tim 1:4), had a timid disposition (1 Cor 16:10–11), and was esteemed highly by the early church (Phil 2:22). The two letters in Scripture that Paul wrote to Timothy were written during Timothy's time overseeing the church in Ephesus.

Have them on your heart
If you are going to be effective at calling other people out, then you will need to have them on your heart. "I thank God whom I serve, as did my ancestors, with a clear conscience, as I remember you constantly in my prayers night and day" (2 Tim 1:3-4). Paul carried Timothy in his heart wherever he went because he loved him. When you love someone, you think about them. They aren't out of sight out of mind for you. They are with you, even when you aren't with them.

How do you get someone on your heart? Well, you need to be close to them. You need to be close enough to care about what affects them, their wins and their losses. Paul is close to Timothy—relationally close. He is affectionate towards him, calling him his child on numerous occasions (1 Tim 1:2,1:18, 2 Tim 1:2,2:1). He is wired in to Timothy and what is going on for him: "As I remember your tears, I long to see you, that I may be filled with joy" (2 Tim 1:4). Having someone on your heart is like riding in a sidecar with them. What happens to them happens to you. You get excited at things going well, and you share the weight when things become difficult.

Some time ago I caught up with a mentor of mine and he opened our conversation together with these words: "I've been thinking about you." That stopped me in my tracks. Someone had cared enough to spend their time thinking about me. I was on someone's heart. Incredible. The conversation could have stopped there. Most of the work had been done; I felt loved. But he went on, and I was glad he did. I was eager to hear the thoughts of someone who cared for me. Whatever they were, I knew they would be good. I began to wonder how different the church would be if more conversations began with those words, which are so simple, yet so powerful.

But despite the pure blessing of having someone thinking about you, Paul's heart for Timothy doesn't stop there. It gets practical. For Paul, there are three ways to express your heart for someone:

1. Pray for them. "I remember you constantly in my prayers night and day" (2 Tim 1:3). The closer you are to someone, the more they are on your heart, the more their wins and losses matter to you, and the more you will pray for them. It's pretty straightforward. You will long for God to energise and help them.

2. Tell them they are on your heart. "I remember you constantly in my prayers ... I remember your tears" (2 Tim 1:3-4). Don't just assume they know it. Tell them, and tell them regularly. Tell them you were thinking about them. Tell them you were wondering how they were going.

3. Plan to see them. "I long to see you, that I may be filled with joy" (2 Tim 1:4). While circumstances can prevent people from being together, plan to catch up with them—preferably face-to-face. And, when you do, let them know you enjoy it.

Be personal with them

If you are going to be effective at calling other people out, then you will need to be prepared to be personal with them. There is no other way. Seeing and knowing each other deeply is critical to calling each other out. While people who don't know us can make helpful observations, they are never as powerful as input from those who see us and know us. You can praise someone from a distance, but you need to be close to truly encourage people. The words of our opponents may ring in our ears, but the well-timed words of those who really know us resonate most deeply. This is because the power of words is proportional to the depth of relationship. And as we have seen, being personal, or knowing and being known, is the engine room of relationship.

While Paul plays a fatherly role in his relationship with Timothy, he does not hesitate to be personal with him. He tells Timothy about his sordid past and God's grace to him (1 Tim 1:12-17), he is open about how his opponents have affected him (2 Tim 1:15, 4:10), he shares his personal needs and asks Timothy for help

(2 Tim 4:13). Paul goes public with his life and allows Timothy to know him, and not for some ulterior motive. It isn't a strategic play to further his ministry objectives. He does it because he loves Timothy and he is in relationship with him.

The people around you don't need another expert, they need spiritual brothers and sisters. There is an abundance of experts in our society. Anyone who needs one can track them down. There are academics, life coaches, counsellors, psychologists—all good resources and all helpful in some way. But knowing and being known isn't central to how they roll. Experts live on a one-way street; the majority of the traffic flows from them to you. They aren't family. Family is a two-way street. Always. Most of what God is up to in our lives happens in the context of a family relationship where being personal with each other is unavoidable.

Fight their enemies alongside them

If you are going to be effective at calling other people out, then you will need to be prepared to roll your sleeves up and fight their enemies alongside them. In a fallen world, enemies abound; some of them are outside of us and some are inside us. We all have our own personal kryptonite, that one thing which has extra power over you and always seems to get the better of you. You can be Superman in almost any situation, but when this enemy shows up you turn to water, every time. Our personal enemies neutralise and sideline us. They can stop us from being the person God made us to be and doing the things God has called us to do.

The enemies of our soul have a way of isolating us. They sometimes feel like a pride of lions hunting their prey. They make us easy pickings by separating us from the rest of the herd, perhaps through shame, guilt or fear. So often, our margin for error seems wafer-thin. We have so much potential, yet our ability to keep the enemy at bay seems so fragile, like we could blow it at a moment's notice. And our enemies don't seem to give up easily. They are tenacious. They are wearying and withering. In this kind of battle, this hand-to-hand combat with our nemesis, there is no sweeter sight than the cavalry appearing on the horizon. Brothers and sisters never let each other fight alone. They know each other's weaknesses and they pull in close and fight together when they are under attack. Perhaps they send short messages of encouragement, shoot up regular prayers for us or, even better, they drop in and hear our heart in the midst of the struggle, straighten out some of our thinking, and then remind us who we are. There are many ways to fight alongside someone else.

Paul knew the importance of this too. In his letters we see him join Timothy in fighting his enemies. He tells Timothy not to listen to those who say he is too young (1 Tim 4:12), he speaks directly into Timothy's fears by reminding him who God has made him to be (2 Tim 1:7), he helps Timothy to be wise about how he executes his responsibilities (1 Tim 2–3, 1 Tim 5), and he skills him up to walk through potential minefields in the church (2 Tim 2:22–26). Paul doesn't sugar-coat reality. He tells Timothy how it is (2 Tim 3:1–9), but he doesn't leave him on his own.

A little while ago, some friends of ours had a rather traumatic weekend. They were expecting their first child and, though everything seemed to be progressing smoothly, on this particular weekend it all started heading south. It looked like the wife was having a miscarriage. Although they were a married couple, it was a grievous situation that each of them had to grapple with in their own way. Suffering had come to their door and it threatened to dehumanise them and their child. The husband was ready to go. He was in the saddle, feeling as many jolts as he could, keen to fight alongside his wife. She, on the other hand, was much closer to the action. It was much deeper and much more personal for her. She had work to do. Early on, she tried to be strong, but it betrayed what was really going on inside. In her effort to be strong, she had begun to disappear and her husband struggled to see her. Her need to be strong had become a kind of invisibility cloak. But then, as they neared the hospital, she began to emerge. She became emotional. As her husband recounted the story, he said it was at that moment he thought, "There you are." A battle was raging, but she needed to let him in on it. He needed to be able to see her in order to fight the battle with her.

Be clear about who they are and what God is calling them to do

If you are going to be effective at calling other people out, then you need to be clear about who they are and what God is calling them to do. In God's family, there is a connection between how he has made us and what he wants us to do. "For we are his workmanship, created in Christ Jesus for good works, which God prepared beforehand, that we should walk in them" (Eph 2:10). Paul is very clear about what God has called Timothy to do, and he repeatedly exhorts him to go after it. Paul highlighted the prophecies about Timothy (1 Tim 1:18), he reminded him he had gifts to use (1 Tim 4:14), he instructed him to preach the word (2 Tim 4:1–2), and he helped him to focus (1 Tim 1:5). Paul knew Timothy, he knew the good works God had called him to do, and he frequently drew his attention to them. Who plays this role in your life? For whom do you play this role?

Let me tell you about a bad day. It was a Tuesday, just over halfway through 2020. It began with some unhelpful criticism that eventually trickled into the struggles going on between me and God. Before long, the trickle became a wicked brew and it went from a bad day to the kind of day that makes pastors wonder about what other job they could do. I made it to the end of the day and went to bed hoping for a better day on Wednesday. I slept fine. The next morning, shortly after waking up, I saw there was a message from Rob, a close spiritual brother of mine who knows something of who I am and what God has called me to do. He wrote, "Felt the need to get up a little early and pray for the work. Stay strong brother. This book and the program that may come from it are important.

Many will be blessed by it." The timestamp on the message was 4:02 AM. It was so powerful. In four short sentences, he cleared the fog of the previous day. It was like he put a hand on either side of my face and turned it back in the right direction. He didn't know about my previous day, but God did, and he used Rob to keep me on track. The world needs more Robs.

It is possible some of you may have some misgivings at this point. You hesitate because you lack clarity on who you are and what God has for you to do. You may even be thinking, "I'm not even clear on what *I* am supposed to be doing, let alone what other people should be doing. How can I be helpful to them if I don't even have my own stuff together?" While I hear you loud and clear, allow me to clarify something. God's helping of us and our helping others are not meant to be linear, sequential events. They will normally happen in parallel. We don't need to get our mess in order before we can help others. Quite the opposite. God means for us to help each other in our unfinished states. If you sit around navel-gazing in an effort to solve all your problems, they will only end up becoming bigger and more intimidating. Your problems will swallow you alive if you let them. But focus on God and other people, curve away from yourself, and you may well find your "healing shall spring up speedily" (Isa 58:6–8). It may be that you find the resolution to your problems when you are not looking for it.

Foster their relationship with God

If you are going to be effective at calling people out, then you will need to actively foster their relationship with God. While this dynamic has been a key focus of this book, it is worth mentioning again briefly. It is only in close communion with God that we become our true selves. We can be bits and pieces of ourselves when we are disconnected from God, but we are never our true selves. When we come close to God, the things which fragment and dehumanise us are banished, and the light and life of God flows in. Our brothers and sisters will never be more who God created them to be than when he is in the centre of their lives.

Paul takes a keen interest in fostering Timothy's relationship with God. He cautions him about distractions (1 Tim 4:6–10), encourages Timothy to fight the good fight of the faith (1 Tim 6:11–16), and calls Timothy to follow him, just as Paul follows Jesus (2 Tim 1:13). Timothy's relationship with God is a critical component in him becoming the person God has made him to be and doing the work God had given him to do.

Run interference on their fears

If you are going to be effective at calling people out, then you will need to run interference on their fears. Fears abound outside the garden. It is, after all, a dangerous world. At the fall, human nature and creation were both broken by sin, and this, combined with our inability to predict the future, makes life risky. Fear is the human response to danger, it helps us prepare to engage with it. But, while fear can be helpful, it often takes things too far and begins to dominate our lives.

Fear is a false prophet, and it turns those who are gripped by it into false prophets.[122] It is a liar; it tells us the thing we fear will certainly happen unless we do something. When we buy the lie sold to us by fear and mix it with the need to control all possible negative outcomes, we become less personal and disappear relationally. No longer are we those exercising our God-given dominion under his rule; we have become our own gods in an effort to control the future and avoid all risk.

To make matters worse, God doesn't seem particularly interested in leading us to a place devoid of fear. Quite to the contrary, he often leads us right into it. Take Timothy, for example. God took him directly to a place that would press his buttons. He was a young (1 Tim 4:12), timid man (1 Cor 16:10–11) who God had sent to lead a church battling with false teachers. On the surface, it doesn't seem to make sense. But there is a sublime logic to it.

God regularly leads his people into situations they can't handle on their own. God called Moses to lead the people out of Egypt (Exod 3), he called Joshua to conquer the promised land (Josh 1), and Jesus led his disciples right into the storm on the sea of Galilee (Mark 4:35–41). None of them could handle the situation on their own. God knows it. It is all part of the plan. At no point has he ever said, nor will he ever say, "Come on, you can do it. You are really savvy. You have what it takes." When we cry out to him and say, "I can't do it. This is too big for me!" He says, "Yep it is. You can't do it. You don't have what it takes. But I will be with you. We will do it together." God is far more interested in partnering with us than inflating our self-esteem.

Expect Jesus to lead you towards what you and he can do together, not what you can do on your own. You won't have what it takes to do what he wants you to do. The task will be too hard, too big, and too powerful. But don't let it scare you. It's all part of the process. If you run from your fears, you will have to keep running, harder and harder, faster and faster. Face up to your fears, with Jesus by your side, and you will defang them and discover God's resourcing in the midst of it. Fear is the gym in which God teaches you to trust him and partner with him more deeply.

Paul runs interference on Timothy's fears. He doesn't let them have the run of the house. He knows how powerful they are in distracting people from who he is and what God has called him to. So, he tells him not to let anyone look down on him because he is young (1 Tim 4:12)—"Don't be intimidated, Timothy." He warns him to stay strong to what he had been taught and not be swayed by false teachers (1 Tim 6:20–21)—"Don't let them get in your head, Timothy." And he reminds him how God has made him powerful (2 Tim 1:6–7)—"Fear is not the most native thing to you now, Timothy. Power, love, and self-control are."

Someone in your corner

What you and I need is someone in our corner. Someone with a voice which will cut through the external and internal noise. Someone who knows us and loves us. We need someone who can see what we face and stare it down with us. Someone who is behind us all the way. While Jesus does this directly, he has organised to deliver a significant portion of his sweet work through other people.

In some ways, we are all Timothys. Every Timothy needs a Paul. Every Timothy needs a few Pauls. Everyone needs people around them who will help them to emerge, to become truly human.

Where are you going to find someone like that?

Perhaps it isn't a question for you. Perhaps it is a question for the people around you.

Where are other people going to find someone like that?

Now you have a question to answer.

That one's for you.

> *Encourage one another and build one another up,*
> *just as you are doing. (1 Thess 5:11)*

Scripture reading
Genesis 15, 1 & 2 Timothy

For reflection and discussion

1. When do you go invisible? What do you do when you become invisible?

2. Where can you see a connection between the times you go invisible and your dehumanisation?

3. Which people truly see you? How does God see you? When do you sense it?

4. Whom do you 'see'? How does your seeing of them help them to become visible?

5. Which elements of encouragement do you want to strengthen in order to be a more encouraging person? Encouragement:
   a. Stirs people to action
   b. Has staying power
   c. Aligns well with the way we have been made
   d. Requires proximity
   e. Is intentional

6. Outside of your immediate family, who is on your heart? Why are they on your heart? What do you do with that?

7. Who fights your enemies with you? How do they do it? With whom do you join in fighting their enemies?

8. Whose fears do you know? How do you run interference on them?

A final word

If you started reading this book with the expectation you would discover some tools or strategies which you could use to bring about your own restoration, then you are probably a little disappointed. I haven't offered you very many. While there is no end to the tips, tricks, hacks, maxims, strategies and self-help systems on offer in our culture, the change you and I need runs far deeper than the self-help section of our local bookstore. It's not that you can't do things more wisely or find new ways to improve your life. It's just that the deepest, most satisfying restoration, the stuff you and I most deeply long for, is well beyond surface level tweaks.

My goal in writing this book wasn't about the development of a system which you could implement to make your life go better; it was about giving you a person. Our human tendency is to look for systems to fix ourselves. Systems allow us to be in control, to be self-made people. We erroneously think that all we need is a little advice or help and we will be fine. But we won't. As relational worshippers, what we most deeply need is a person, the person of Jesus. Jesus, the true human, is the one who makes you truly human. In all likelihood, you probably already knew him when you started reading this book, but it is my hope that he is a little closer to you now. Hopefully, the truth you always knew is just a little bit more personal.

I want to finish by making something explicit which, in one way or another, has been largely implicit throughout this book. It has been the overarching principle and backbone of everything you have read. This is it:

> *You don't find yourself by looking for yourself.*
> *You find yourself when you find Jesus.*

It's simply how it works. Becoming truly human is dependent upon you being connected to the true human—Jesus. And you can't be connected to him unless you put your self to death.

> *For whoever would save his life will lose it,*
> *but whoever loses his life for my sake will find it.*
> *(Matt 16:25)*

It's the great irony. Die to yourself, and you will find your true self. Grasp after your self and you will lose your true self. And it holds true, not just in an ultimate sense, but in a lived sense, day by day. Any striving to be great in our own right, any striving to discover ourselves without Jesus, any defiant pride affirming our significance, will only end in our lives slipping like sand through our fingers. But die to yourself, and connect to the one who is light and life, and you will find your true self. It is only then you become truly human.

To continue the journey visit www.becomingyou.com.au

References

Augustine, St. *Teaching Christianity*. New York: New City Press, 1996.

Augustine, St. *The Confessions of St. Augustine*. Translated by J G Pilkington. Edinburgh: T. & T. Clark, 1876.

Backus, W. *The Hidden Rift with God*. Minneapolis, MN: Bethany House Publishers, 1990.

Beale, G K. *The Temple and the Church's Mission – a Biblical Theology of the Dwelling Place of God*. New Studies in Biblical Theology. Edited by D A Carson. Downers Grove, IL: Intervarsity Press, 2004.

———. *We Become What We Worship: A Biblical Theology of Idolatry*. Downers Grove, IL: InterVarsity Press, 2008.

Beale, G K, and M Kim. *God Dwells among Us – Expanding Eden to the Ends of the Earth*. Downers Grover, IL: Intervarsity Press, 2014.

Best, H M. *Unceasing Worship: Biblical Perpsectives on Worship and the Arts*. Downers Grove, IL: Intervarsity Press, 2003.

Cacioppo, J T, and W Patrick. *Loneliness: Human Nature and the Need for Social Connection*. New York, NY: W. W. Norton & Company, 2008.

Calvin, J. *Commentaries on the Epistles of Paul to the Galatians and the Ephesians*. Translated by Rev. William Pringle. Edinburgh: The Calvin Translation Society, 1854.

———. *Commentary Upon the Acts of the Apostles*. Translated by Henry Beveridge. Vol. II, Grand Rapids, MI: Baker Book House, 1993.

———. *Institutes of the Christian Religion*. Translated by H Beveridge. Peabody, MA: Hendrickson Publishers, 2008.

———. *Institutes of the Christian Religion* Edinburgh: The Calvin Translation Society, 1845.

Oxford Dictionary of Modern Quotations. Third ed. Oxford: Oxford University Press, 2007.

Canlis, J. *Calvin's Ladder: A Spiritual Theology of Ascent and Ascension*. Grand Rapids, MI: Wm. B. Eerdmans Publishing Co., 2010.

Carson, Don A. *The Gospel According to John*. The Pillar New Testament Commentary. Leicester England, Grand Rapids, MI: InterVarsity Press, W. B. Eerdmans, 1991.

Edwards, James R. *The Gospel According to Luke*. The Pillar New Testament Commentary. Grand Rapids, MI, Cambridge, U.K., Nottingham, England: William B. Eerdmans Publishing Company, Apollos, 2015.

———. *The Gospel According to Mark*. The Pillar New Testament Commentary. Grand Rapids, MI, Leicester, England: Eerdmans, Apollos, 2002.

The Ellen DeGeneres Show. Season 8, episode 152. Produced by Chris Cavell, Ellen DeGeneres, Kevin A. Leman II, Beth Sherman. Aired April 28, 2011, on NBC.

Emerson, R W. *Society and Solitude.* Cambridge: Riverside Press, 1883.

Frame, J M. *The Doctrine of the Christian Life: A Theology of Lordship.* Phillipsburg, NJ: P & R Publishing, 2008.

———. *Systematic Theology: An Introduction to Christian Belief.* Phillipsburg, NJ: P&R Publishing, 2013.

Griffiths, A, and T Denton. *Professor Stupido: The Greatest Un–Inventor in the World.* Little Treehouse. Sydney, New South Wales, Australia: Pan Macmillan Australia Pty Ltd, 2020.

Hamilton, V P. *The Book of Genesis: Chapters 1–17.* New International Commentary on the Old Testament. Grand Rapids, MI: Eerdmans Publishing Company, 1990.

Jackson, P. "The Return of the King." In *The Lord of the Rings*, edited by P Jackson, 192 minutes: New Line Productions, Inc., 2003.

Keller, T. *The Freedom of Self-Forgetfulness.* UK: 10 Publishing, 2012. Kindle.

Knight, G. *The Magical World of the Inklings.* Cheltenham, England: Skylight Press, 2010.

Korgen, K, and J M White. *The Engaged Sociologist: Connecting the Classroom to the Community.* Thousand Oaks, CA: Pine Forge Press, 2007.

Lewis, C S. *The Complete Works of C S Lewis.* E–Artnow, 2016. Kindle.

Liefeld, Walter L. *Luke.* The Expositor's Bible Commentary: Matthew, Mark, Luke. Edited by Frank E Gaebelein. Vol. 8, Grand Rapids, MI: Zondervan Publishing House, 1984.

Lucado, M. *A Love Worth Giving: Living in the Overflow of God's Love.* Nashville, TN: Thomas Nelson, 2002.

Morris, Leon. *The Gospel According to John*. New International Commentary on the New Testament. Grand Rapids, MI: Eerdmans Publishing Co., 1995.

New International Version. Grand Rapids, MI: Zondervan, 2011.

Peterson, Eugene H. *Christ Plays in Ten Thousand Places*. Grand Rapids, MI: Wm. B. Eerdmans Publishing Co. Kindle.

———. *The Message Remix: The Bible in Contemporary Language*. Colorado Springs, CO: NavPress Publishing Group, 2006.

———. *Practice Resurrection: A Conversation on Growing up in Christ*. Grand Rapids, MI, Cambridge, UK: William B. Eerdmans Publishing Company, 2010. Kindle.

Piff, P K, M Feinberg, P Dietze, D M Stancato, and D Keltner. "Awe, the Small Self, and Prosocial Behavior." *Journal of Personality and Social Psychology* 108, no. 6 (2015): 883–99.

Plantinga, Cornelius Jr. *Not the Way It's Supposed to Be: A Breviary of Sin*. Grand Rapids, MI: Wm. B. Eerdmans Publishing Co., 1995.

Powlison, David. "Idols of the Heart and 'Vanity Fair'." *The Journal of Biblical Counselling* 13, no. 2 (1995): 35–50.

Reist, M T. "Self Love." Australian Broadcasting Corporation, https://www.abc.net.au/news/2010-03-18/33222.

Rosner, B S. *Known by God: A Biblical Theology of Personal Identity*. Biblical Theology for Life. Edited by J Lunde. Grand Rapids, MI: Zondervan, 2017.

Sailhammer, J H. *Genesis*. The Expositors Bible Commentary: Genesis, Exodus, Leviticus, Numbers. Edited by F E Gaebelein. Vol. 2, Grand Rapids, MI: Zondervan Publishing House, 1990.

Schopenhauer, A. *Parerga and Paralippomena*. Translated by E F J Payne. Vol. 1, New York: Oxford University Press, 1974.

Scott Duvall, J, and J Daniel Hays. *God's Relational Presence: The Cohesive Center of Biblical Theology*. Grand Rapids, MI: Baker Academic, 2019.

Seagal, M. "Believer, Become What You Are." Desiring God, https://www.desiringgod.org/articles/believer-become-what-you-are.

Slater, T. *Beauty and the Beast*. New York, NY: Golden Books, 2004. Kindle.

Thoreau, H D. *Walden*. Boston: James R. Osgood and Company, 1878.

Tolkien, J R R. *The Fellowship of the Ring*. The Lord of the Rings. London: Harper Collins Publishers, 1966.

Tripp, P D. *Dangerous Calling: Confronting the Unique Challenges of Pastoral Ministry*. Wheaton, Ill: Crossway, 2012.

———. *Instruments in the Redeemer's Hands: How to Help Others Change – Facilitator's Guide*. Greensboro, NC: New Growth Press, 2010.

———. *Instruments in the Redeemers Hands*. NJ: P&R Publishing, 2002.

VanGemeren, W A. "Psalms." In *The Expositors Bible Commentary: Psalms, Proverbs, Ecclesiastes, Song of Songs*, edited by F E Gaebelien. Grand Rapids, MI: Zondervan Publishing House, 1991.

Walton, J H. *Genesis*. New International Version Appplication Commentary. Grand Rapids, MI: Zondervan, 2001.

Welch, E T. *Addictions a Banquet in the Grave: Finding Hope in the Power of the Gospel*. Greensboro, NC: New Growth Press, 2011.

———. *Depression: Looking up from the Stubborn Darkness*. Greensboro, NC: New Growth Press, 2012. Kindle.

———. *Running Scared: Fear, Worry, and the God of Rest.* Greensboro, NC: New Growth Press, 2007.

———. *Shame Interrupted: How God Lifts the Pain or Worthlessness and Rejection.* Greensboro, NC: New Growth Press, 2012. Kindle.

———. *Side by Side: Walking with Others in Wisdom and Love.* Wheaton, IL: Crossway, 2015.

Wenham, G J. *Genesis 1–15.* Vol. 1, Dallas: Word, Incorporated, 1987.

———. *Genesis 16–50.* Word Biblical Commentary. Edited by D A Hubbard and G W Barker. Vol. 2, Dallas, TX: Word Incorporated, 1994.

Wilbourne, Rankin. *Union with Christ: The Way to Know and Enjoy God.* Colorado Springs, CO: David C Cook, 2016.

Wood, D R W, I H Marshall, A R Millard, J I Packer, and D J Wiseman, eds. *New Bible Dictionary.* 3rd ed. Leicester, England: InterVarsity Press, 1996.

Yarbrough, R W. *The Letters to Timothy and Titus.* Pillar New Testament Commentary. Edited by D A Carson. Grand Rapids, MI: William B Eerdmands Publishing Company, 2018.

Endnotes

1. Cornelius Jr. Plantinga, *Not the Way It's Supposed to Be: A Breviary of Sin* (Grand Rapids, MI: Wm. B. Eerdmans Publishing Co., 1995), 10.

2. Ibid., 7.

3. J Scott Duvall and J Daniel Hays, *God's Relational Presence: The Cohesive Center of Biblical Theology* (Grand Rapids, MI: Baker Academic, 2019), 15.

4. J H Walton, Genesis, *New International Version Appplication Commentary* (Grand Rapids, MI: Zondervan, 2001), 182.

5. G J Wenham, *Genesis 1–15*, vol. 1 (Dallas: Word, Incorporated, 1987), 86.

6. D R W Wood et al., eds., *New Bible Dictionary*, 3rd ed. (Leicester, England: InterVarsity Press, 1996), 266.

7. J M Frame, *Systematic Theology: An Introduction to Christian Belief* (Phillipsburg, NJ: P&R Publishing, 2013), 858–59.

8. Scott Duvall and Daniel Hays, *God's Relational Presence: The Cohesive Center of Biblical Theology*, 19.

9. Ibid., 13.

10   E T Welch, *Shame Interrupted: How God Lifts the Pain or Worthlessness and Rejection*, (Greensboro, NC: New Growth Press, 2012). Kindle. loc. 142–46.

11   H D Thoreau, Walden (Boston: James R. Osgood and Company, 1878), 10.

12   Hebrews 4:5 - Eugene H Peterson, *The Message Remix: The Bible in Contemporary Language* (Colorado Springs, CO: NavPress Publishing Group, 2006).

13   Welch, *Shame Interrupted: How God Lifts the Pain or Worthlessness and Rejection*. loc. 536-37.

14   For example Ezekiel 37:26–27.

15   Scott Duvall and Daniel Hays, *God's Relational Presence: The Cohesive Center of Biblical Theology*, 133.

16   G K Beale and M Kim, *God Dwells among Us – Expanding Eden to the Ends of the Earth* (Downers Grover, IL: Intervarsity Press, 2014), 8.

17   G K Beale, *The Temple and the Church's Mission – a Biblical Theology of the Dwelling Place of God*, ed. D A Carson, New Studies in Biblical Theology (Downers Grove, IL: Intervarsity Press, 2004), 67; Beale and Kim, *God Dwells among Us – Expanding Eden to the Ends of the Earth*.

18   Beale, *The Temple and the Church's Mission – a Biblical Theology of the Dwelling Place of God*, 67.

19   P K Piff et al., "Awe, the Small Self, and Prosocial Behavior," *Journal of Personality and Social Psychology 108*, no. 6 (2015).

20   E Cammaerts, in *Oxford Dictionary of Modern Quotations*, ed. Elizabeth Knowles (Oxford: Oxford University Press, 2007).

21   H M Best, *Unceasing Worship: Biblical Perpsectives on Worship and the Arts* (Downers Grove, IL: Intervarsity Press, 2003), 17.

22   Names and identifying details of the personal stories included in this book have been changed in order to protect anonymity.

23   C S Lewis, *The Complete Works of C S Lewis*, (E-Artnow, 2016). Kindle. loc. 43518–19.

24   *The Ellen DeGeneres Show*, season 8, episode 152, directed by

Suzanne Luna and Liz Patrick, aired April 28 2011 on NBC.

25 Beale and Kim, *God Dwells among Us – Expanding Eden to the Ends of the Earth*, 26.

26 J Calvin, *Institutes of the Christian Religion*, trans. H Beveridge (Peabody, MA: Hendrickson Publishers, 2008), 128.

27 *Commentary Upon the Acts of the Apostles*, trans. Henry Beveridge, vol. II (Grand Rapids, MI: Baker Book House, 1993), 413.

28 David Powlison, "Idols of the Heart and 'Vanity Fair'", *The Journal of Biblical Counselling 13*, no. 2 (1995): 36.

29 E T Welch, *Side by Side: Walking with Others in Wisdom and Love* (Wheaton, IL: Crossway, 2015), 11.

30 J Canlis, *Calvin's Ladder: A Spiritual Theology of Ascent and Ascension* (Grand Rapids, MI: Wm. B. Eerdmans Publishing Co., 2010), 69.

31 C S Lewis, *The Complete Works of C S Lewis*. loc. 53993–94.

32 Ibid., loc. 56120–22.

33 Ibid., loc. 51851.

34 J R R Tolkien, *The Fellowship of the Ring, The Lord of the Rings* (London: Harper Collins Publishers, 1966), 71.

35 Ibid., 70.

36 Ibid., 73.

37 P Jackson, "The Return of the King", ibid., ed. P Jackson (New Line Productions, Inc., 2003).

38 G K Beale, *We Become What We Worship: A Biblical Theology of Idolatry* (Downers Grove, IL: InterVarsity Press, 2008), 12.

39 Ibid., 16.

40 St Augustine, *Teaching Christianity* (New York: New City Press, 1996), 118.

41 M T Reist, "Self Love", Australian Broadcasting Corporation, https://www.abc.net.au/news/2010-03-18/33222.

42 Ibid.

43 E T Welch, *Addictions a Banquet in the Grave: Finding Hope in the Power of the Gospel* (Greensboro, NC: New Growth Press, 2011), 46.

44 Powlison, "Idols of the Heart and 'Vanity Fair'", 42.

45 Frame, *Systematic Theology: An Introduction to Christian Belief*, 38.

46 Ibid.

47 Canlis, *Calvin's Ladder: A Spiritual Theology of Ascent and Ascension*, 69.

48 Eugene H Peterson, *Christ Plays in Ten Thousand Places*, (Grand Rapids, MI: Wm. B. Eerdmans Publishing Co.). Kindle. 325–26.

49 Best, *Unceasing Worship: Biblical Perpsectives on Worship and the Arts*, 20.

50 J Calvin, *Institutes of the Christian Religion* (Edinburgh: The Calvin Translation Society, 1845). 163.

51 P D Tripp, *Instruments in the Redeemer's Hands: How to Help Others Change – Facilitator's Guide* (Greensboro, NC: New Growth Press, 2010), 28.

52 T Slater, *Beauty and the Beast*, (New York, NY: Golden Books, 2004). Kindle.

53 Ibid., loc. 4.

54 I will refer to them collectively as Israel.

55 Peterson, *The Message Remix: The Bible in Contemporary Language*, 1299.

56 Ibid.

57 G Knight, *The Magical World of the Inklings* (Cheltenham, England: Skylight Press, 2010), 9.

58 Ibid., 19.

59 Ibid., 16.

60 Lewis, *The Complete Works of C S Lewis*. loc. 16838–40.

61 Ibid., loc. 16992–93.

62 Ibid., loc. 16993–7002.

63 A Griffiths and T Denton, *Professor Stupido: The Greatest Un-Inventor in the World, Little Treehouse* (Sydney, New South Wales, Australia: Pan Macmillan Australia Pty Ltd, 2020).

64 Ibid., 44.

65 Ibid., 58.

66 Leon Morris, *The Gospel According to John*, New International Commentary on the New Testament (Grand Rapids, MI: Eerdmans Publishing Co., 1995), 118.

67 Wood et al., *New Bible Dictionary*, 754.

68 Don A Carson, *The Gospel According to John, The Pillar New Testament Commentary* (Leicester England, Grand Rapids, MI: Inter-Varsity Press, W. B. Eerdmans, 1991), 156.

69 J Calvin, *Commentaries on the Epistles of Paul to the Galatians and the Ephesians*, trans. Rev. William Pringle (Edinburgh: The Calvin Translation Society, 1854), 140.

70 St. Augustine, *The Confessions of St. Augustine*, trans. J G Pilkington (Edinburgh: T. & T. Clark, 1876), 1.

71 James R Edwards, *The Gospel According to Luke, The Pillar New Testament Commentary* (Grand Rapids, MI, Cambridge, U.K., Nottingham, England: William B. Eerdmans Publishing Company, Apollos, 2015), 529.

72 Walter L Liefeld, *Luke*, ed. Frank E Gaebelein, vol. 8, *The Expositor's Bible Commentary: Matthew, Mark, Luke* (Grand Rapids, MI: Zondervan Publishing House, 1984), 1007.

73 Lewis, *The Complete Works of C S Lewis*. loc. 52462–65.

74 Calvin, *Institutes of the Christian Religion*, Vol.2, 1.

75 Canlis, *Calvin's Ladder: A Spiritual Theology of Ascent and Ascension*, 90.

76 James R Edwards, *The Gospel According to Mark, The Pillar New Testament Commentary* (Grand Rapids, MI, Leicester, England: Eerdmans, Apollos, 2002), 68.

77 Scott Duvall and Daniel Hays, *God's Relational Presence: The Cohesive Center of Biblical Theology*, 258.

78 Ibid., 226.

79 Lewis, *The Complete Works of C S Lewis*. loc. 13905–06.

80 Eugene H Peterson, *Practice Resurrection: A Conversation on Growing up in Christ*, (Grand Rapids, MI, Cambridge, UK: William B. Eerdmans Publishing Company, 2010). Kindle. loc. 52–54.

81 Carson, *The Gospel According to John*, 190.

82 Peterson, *Practice Resurrection: A Conversation on Growing up in Christ*. loc. 58–62.

83 Lewis, *The Complete Works of C S Lewis*. loc. 52432-36.

84 J T Cacioppo and W Patrick, *Loneliness: Human Nature and the Need for Social Connection* (New York, NY: W. W. Norton & Company, 2008), 3.

85 Scott Duvall and Daniel Hays, *God's Relational Presence: The Cohesive Center of Biblical Theology*, 294.

86 V P Hamilton, *The Book of Genesis: Chapters 1–17*, New International Commentary on the Old Testament (Grand Rapids, MI: Eerdmans Publishing Company, 1990), 220.

87 B S Rosner, *Known by God: A Biblical Theology of Personal Identity*, ed. J Lunde, Biblical Theology for Life (Grand Rapids, MI: Zondervan, 2017), 94.

88 Scott Duvall and Daniel Hays, *God's Relational Presence: The Cohesive Center of Biblical Theology*, 280.

89 A phrase I have drawn from Eugene Peterson's writings.

90 Rankin Wilbourne, *Union with Christ: The Way to Know and Enjoy God* (Colorado Springs, CO: David C Cook, 2016), 85.

91 Welch, *Shame Interrupted: How God Lifts the Pain or Worthlessness and Rejection*. loc. 142–46.

92 W Backus, *The Hidden Rift with God* (Minneapolis, MN: Bethany House Publishers, 1990).

93 Frame, *Systematic Theology: An Introduction to Christian Belief*, 37.

94 Be careful not to take this one too far. It is a two-way street. Loving another often requires that we forgo what we desire for the betterment of another. I intentionally chose an outlandish example to illustrate the underlying dynamic of responding to someone's likes and dislikes in relationship.

95 W A VanGemeren, "Psalms," in *The Expositors Bible Commentary: Psalms, Proverbs, Ecclesiastes, Song of Songs*, ed. F E Gaebelien (Grand Rapids, MI: Zondervan Publishing House, 1991), 5.

96 Canlis, *Calvin's Ladder: A Spiritual Theology of Ascent and Ascension*, 115.

97 Peterson, *Practice Resurrection: A Conversation on Growing up in Christ*. loc. 910–11.

98 M Seagal, "Believer, Become What You Are," Desiring God, https://www.desiringgod.org/articles/believer-become-what-you-are.

99 P D Tripp, *Dangerous Calling: Confronting the Unique Challenges of Pastoral Ministry* (Wheaton, Ill: Crossway, 2012), 194.

100 E T Welch, *Depression: Looking up from the Stubborn Darkness*, (Greensboro, NC: New Growth Press, 2012). Kindle. loc. 1345.

101 J M Frame, *The Doctrine of the Christian Life: A Theology of Lordship* (Phillipsburg, NJ: P & R Publishing, 2008), 253.

102 Scott Duvall and Daniel Hays, *God's Relational Presence: The Cohesive Center of Biblical Theology*.

103 Frame, *The Doctrine of the Christian Life: A Theology of Lordship*, 252.

104 Beale, *We Become What We Worship: A Biblical Theology of Idolatry*.

105 A Schopenhauer, *Parerga and Paralippomena*, trans. E F J Payne, vol. 1 (New York: Oxford University Press, 1974), 397.

106 K Korgen and J M White, *The Engaged Sociologist: Connecting the Classroom to the Community* (Thousand Oaks, CA: Pine Forge Press, 2007), 58. M Lucado, *A Love Worth Giving: Living in the Overflow of God's Love* (Nashville, TN: Thomas Nelson, 2002), 133.

107 T Keller, *The Freedom of Self-Forgetfulness*, (UK: 10 Publishing, 2012). Kindle. loc. 262–63.

108 Peterson, *Practice Resurrection: A Conversation on Growing up in Christ*. loc. 910–11.

109 P D Tripp, *Instruments in the Redeemer's Hands* (NJ: P&R Publishing, 2002), 41.

110 Canlis, *Calvin's Ladder: A Spiritual Theology of Ascent and Ascension*, 150.

111 Calvin, *Institutes of the Christian Religion* 415.

112 Tripp, *Instruments in the Redeemer's Hands*, 40.

113 R W Emerson, *Society and Solitude* (Cambridge: Riverside Press, 1883), 276.

114 Tripp, *Dangerous Calling: Confronting the Unique Challenges of Pastoral Ministry*, 23.

115 New International Version, (Grand Rapids, MI: Zondervan, 2011).

116 G J Wenham, *Genesis 16–50*, ed. D A Hubbard and G W Barker, vol. 2, *Word Biblical Commentary* (Dallas, TX: Word Incorporated, 1994). J H Sailhammer, *Genesis*, ed. F E Gaebelein, vol. 2, *The Expositors Bible Commentary: Genesis, Exodus, Leviticus, Numbers* (Grand Rapids, MI: Zondervan Publishing House, 1990).

117 Genesis, 2, 134.

118 Wenham, Genesis 16–50, 2, 8.

119 Sailhammer, Genesis, 2, 134.

120 Wenham, Genesis 16–50, 2, 9.

121 R W Yarbrough, *The Letters to Timothy and Titus*, ed. D A Carson, Pillar New Testament Commentary (Grand Rapids, MI: William B Eerdmands Publishing Company, 2018), 53.

122 E T Welch, *Running Scared: Fear, Worry, and the God of Rest* (Greensboro, NC: New Growth Press, 2007), 52.

www.ingramcontent.com/pod-product-compliance
Lightning Source LLC
Chambersburg PA
CBHW050309010526
44107CB00055B/2165